16LIVES

SEÁN HEUSTON

JOHN GIBNEY – AUTHOR OF 16LIVES: SEÁN HEUSTON

John Gibney is a graduate of Trinity College, Dublin. He is the author of *Ireland and the Popish Plot* (Palgrave Macmillan, 2008) and *The shadow of a year: the 1641 rebellion in Irish history and memory* (University of Wisconsin Press, 2013). He was a contributor to the Royal Irish Academy's *Dictionary of Irish Biography* (Cambridge University Press, 2009), and was the producer of the acclaimed RTE Radio 1 documentary on historical Dublin street gangs, *The Animal Gangs*. He has also been a research fellow at the University of Notre Dame and at NUI Galway. Originally from Kilbarrack in north Dublin, he has worked in heritage tourism in the city since 2001.

- -

LORCAN COLLINS – SERIES EDITOR

Lorcan Collins was born and raised in Dublin. A lifelong interest in history led to the foundation of his hugely-popular 1916 Walking Tour in 1996. He co-authored *The Easter Rising: A Guide to Dublin in 1916* (O'Brien Press, 2000) with Conor Kostick. His biography of James Connolly was published in the *16 Lives* series in 2012. He is also a regular contributor to radio, television and historical journals. *16 Lives* is Lorcan's concept and he is co-editor of the series.

DR RUÁN O'DONNELL – SERIES EDITOR

Dr Ruán O'Donnell is a senior lecturer at the University of Limerick. A graduate of University College Dublin and the Australian National University, O'Donnell has published extensively on Irish Republicanism. Titles include *Robert Emmet and the Rising of 1803*, *The Impact of 1916* (editor) and *Special Category, The IRA in English prisons 1968–1978* and *The O'Brien Pocket History of the Irish Famine*. He is a director of the Irish Manuscript Commission and a frequent contributor to the national and international media on the subject of Irish revolutionary history.

16 LIVES
SEÁN HEUSTON

John Gibney

**Waterford City and County
Libraries**

THE O'BRIEN PRESS
DUBLIN

First published 2013 by
The O'Brien Press Ltd,
12 Terenure Road East, Rathgar,
Dublin 6, Ireland.
Tel: +353 1 4923333; Fax: +353 1 4922777
E-mail: books@obrien.ie.
Website: www.obrien.ie
ISBN: 978-1-84717-268-6
Text © copyright John Gibney 2013
Copyright for typesetting, layout, editing, design
© The O'Brien Press Ltd
Series concept: Lorcan Collins
British Library Cataloguing-in-Publication Data
A catalogue record for this title is available from the British Library
1 2 3 4 5 6 7 8
13 14 15 16 17

Printed and bound by CPI Group (UK) Ltd, Croydon, CR0 4YY
The paper used in this book is produced using pulp from managed forests

PICTURE CREDITS

The author and publisher thank the following for permission to use photographs and
illustrative material: front cover image: National Library of Ireland (NLI); back cover &
inside front cover: NLI.
Courtesy of Kilmainham Gaol Museum: section 1, p1, p2 top; section 2, p2, top, p4,
top, p5, bottom, p6, bottom, p7, p8. National Library of Ireland: section 1, p2, bottom,
p3 bottom, p4, p6, top & bottom; section 2, p2, bottom, p4, bottom. Courtesy of the
National Museum of Ireland: section 1, p5, top. Eamon Murphy: section 1, p3 top; Jim
Langton Collection: section 1, p5 bottom; Des Long: section 1, p7; Mary Evans Picture
Library: section 1, p8; section 2, p5, bottom; Lorcan Collins: section 2, p1 top & bottom
right, p3 top & bottom; RTÉ: section 2, p1 bottom left; Copyright unknown: section 2,
p6, top; Author's own: section 2, p6 centre.

If any involuntary infringement of copyright has occurred, sincere apologies are offered
and the owners of such copyright are requested to contact the publisher.

ACKNOWLEDGEMENTS

There are a number of people I would like to thank for their assistance with this biography. Lorcan Collins was open to my willingness to tackle Heuston, and both he and Ruán O'Donnell have helped to keep the project on track. Edward Madigan gave me the benefit of his expertise on a number of occasions. I would like to thank the following individuals for generously providing me with leads, sources, and suggestions: Niall Bergin, David Kilmartin, Jim Langton, Damien Lawlor, Des Long, Shane Mac Thomais, Eamon Murphy, Andrias Ó Cathasaigh, Brian Ó Conchubhair, and Jim Stephenson. I would also like to thank Pádraig Óg Ó Ruairc for permitting me to consult the late Donnchadh Ó Shea's unpublished manuscript 'Na Fianna Eireann, 1909-1975'. I naturally wish to thank the staff of the various archives and libraries in which I worked, especially Anne-Marie Ryan, formerly of Kilmainham Gaol; Brother Patrick Brogan of the Allen Library; and Peter Rigney of the Irish Railway Record Society Archives. At O'Brien Press Helen Carr has been an exemplary editor, and the text has benefited enormously from her scrutiny. Finally, I wish to thank my parents, Joan and Charlie, and Liza Costello for their encouragement and patience.

16LIVES Timeline

1845–51. The Great Hunger in Ireland. One million people die and over the next decades millions more emigrate.

1858, March 17. The Irish Republican Brotherhood, or Fenians, are formed with the express intention of overthrowing British rule in Ireland by whatever means necessary.

1867, February and March. Fenian Uprising.

1870, May. Home Rule movement, founded by Isaac Butt, who had previously campaigned for amnesty for Fenian prisoners

1879–81. The Land War. Violent agrarian agitation against English landlords.

1884, November 1. The Gaelic Athletic Association founded – immediately infiltrated by the Irish Republican Brotherhood (IRB).

1893, July 31. Gaelic League founded by Douglas Hyde and Eoin MacNeill. The *Gaelic Revival*, a period of Irish Nationalism, pride in the language, history, culture and sport.

1900, September. *Cumann na nGaedheal* (Irish Council) founded by Arthur Griffith.

1905–07. *Cumann na nGaedheal*, the Dungannon Clubs and the National Council are amalgamated to form *Sinn Féin* (We Ourselves).

1909, August. Countess Markievicz and Bulmer Hobson organise nationalist youths into *Na Fianna Éireann* (Warriors of Ireland) a kind of boy scout brigade.

1912, April. Asquith introduces the Third Home Rule Bill to the British Parliament. Passed by the Commons and rejected by the Lords, the Bill would have to become law due to the Parliament Act. Home Rule expected to be introduced for Ireland by autumn 1914.

1913, January. Sir Edward Carson and James Craig set up Ulster Volunteer Force (UVF) with the intention of defending Ulster against Home Rule.

1913. Jim Larkin, founder of the Irish Transport and General Workers' Union (ITGWU) calls for a workers' strike for better pay and conditions.

1913, August 31. Jim Larkin speaks at a banned rally on Sackville Street; Bloody Sunday.

1913, November 23. James Connolly, Jack White and Jim Larkin establish the Irish Citizen Army (ICA) in order to protect strikers.

1913, November 25. The Irish Volunteers founded in Dublin to 'secure the rights and liberties common to all the people of Ireland'.

1914, March 20. Resignations of British officers force British government not to use British army to enforce Home Rule, an event known as the 'Curragh Mutiny'.

1914, April 2. In Dublin, Agnes O'Farrelly, Mary MacSwiney, Countess Markievicz and others establish Cumann na mBan as a women's volunteer force dedicated to establishing Irish freedom and assisting the Irish Volunteers.

1914, April 24. A shipment of 35,000 rifles and five million rounds of ammunition is landed at Larne for the UVF.

1914, July 26. Irish Volunteers unload a shipment of 900 rifles and 45,000 rounds of ammunition shipped from Germany aboard Erskine Childers' yacht, the *Asgard*. British troops fire on crowd on Bachelors Walk, Dublin. Three citizens are killed.

1914, August 4. Britain declares war on Germany. Home Rule for Ireland shelved for the duration of the First World War.

1914, September 9. Meeting held at Gaelic League headquarters between IRB and other extreme republicans. Initial decision made to stage an uprising while Britain is at war.

1914, September. 170,000 leave the Volunteers and form the National Volunteers or Redmondites. Only 11,000 remain as the Irish Volunteers under Eóin MacNeill.

1915, May–September. Military Council of the IRB is formed.

1915, August 1. Pearse gives fiery oration at the funeral of Jeremiah O'Donovan Rossa.

1916, January 19–22. James Connolly joined the IRB Military Council, thus ensuring that the ICA shall be involved in the Rising. Rising date confirmed for Easter.

1916, April 20, 4.15pm. *The Aud* arrives at Tralee Bay, laden with 20,000 German rifles for the Rising. Captain Karl Spindler waits in vain for a signal from shore.

1916, April 21, 2.15am. Roger Casement and his two companions go ashore from U-19 and land on Banna Strand. Casement is arrested at McKenna's Fort.

6.30pm. *The Aud* is captured by the British navy and forced to sail towards Cork Harbour.

22 April, 9.30am. *The Aud* is scuttled by her captain off Daunt's Rock.

10pm. Eóin MacNeill as chief-of-staff of the Irish Volunteers issues the countermanding order in Dublin to try to stop the Rising.

1916, April 23, 9am, Easter Sunday. The Military Council meets to discuss the situation, considering MacNeill has placed an advertisement in a Sunday newspaper halting all Volunteer operations. The Rising is put on hold for twenty-four hours. Hundreds of copies of *The Proclamation of the Republic* are printed in Liberty Hall.

1916, April 24, 12 noon, Easter Monday. The Rising begins in Dublin.

16LIVESMAP

REBEL POSITIONS
REBEL HELD AREAS
BRITISH CORDON OF TROOPS

FINGLAS R

CABRA ROAD

Phoenix Park

St Brendan's Hospital

NTH BR

FI
BATT

Collins Barracks

Magazine Fort

Heuston Station

James's Gate Brewery

Mendicity Institution

Royal Hospital

JAMES'S ST

Kilmainham Gaol

St James's Hospital (South Dublin Union)

FOURTH BATTALION

SOUTH

CIRCULAR

ROAD

Griffith Barracks

To Kimma

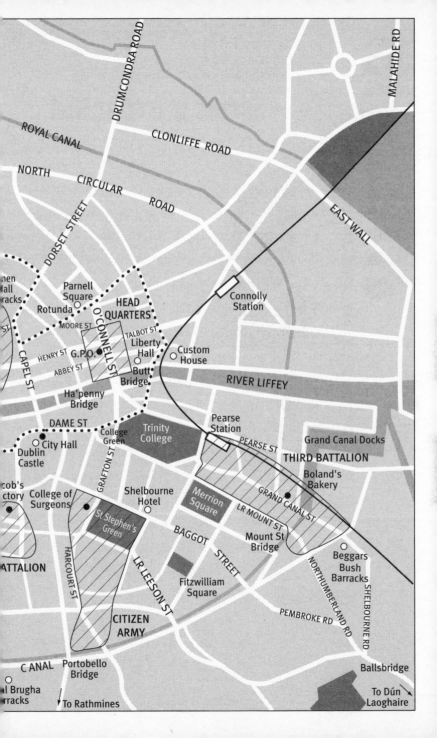

16LIVES – Series Introduction

This book is part of a series called *16 LIVES*, conceived with the objective of recording for posterity the lives of the sixteen men who were executed after the 1916 Easter Rising. Who were these people and what drove them to commit themselves to violent revolution?

The rank and file as well as the leadership were all from diverse backgrounds. Some were privileged and some had no material wealth. Some were highly educated writers, poets or teachers and others had little formal schooling. Their common desire, to set Ireland on the road to national freedom, united them under the one banner of the army of the Irish Republic. They occupied key buildings in Dublin and around Ireland for one week before they were forced to surrender. The leaders were singled out for harsh treatment and all sixteen men were executed for their role in the Rising.

Meticulously researched yet written in an accessible fashion, the *16 LIVES* biographies can be read as individual volumes but together they make a highly collectible series.

Lorcan Collins & Dr Ruán O'Donnell,
16 Lives *Series Editors*

CONTENTS

A note on conventions:

For the sake of clarity, I have adopted a number of conventions in the text and appendices. Differing spellings have been standardised, with the most common form preferred throughout; for example, 'Seán' rather than 'Seaghán', etc. However, as Heuston's family usually referred to him as 'Jack', I have retained this usage in quotations wherever it was used by those closest to him. In quotations, I have silently modernised and standardised punctuation and grammar, and I have indicated interpolations and uncertain words in square brackets. With regards to place names, to avoid confusion I have preferred the terms currently in use, for example, 'O'Connell Street' rather than 'Sackville Street'. The Mendicity Institution is often called the 'Mendicity Institute'. This is incorrect: it was, and remains, the Mendicity Institution. The two terms are used interchangeably in quotations, and I have not standardised these, but I have opted for the term 'institution' in the text itself. Finally, and perhaps most importantly, all dialogue in the text has been taken verbatim from first-hand testimonies: it is reproduced as it was recorded.

Introduction

Seán Heuston wasn't always called Seán. He was baptised 'John Joseph', and to his siblings he was 'Jack'. At some point in his short life he had learnt Irish; in 1901, at the age of ten, he had been the only member of his family to claim any knowledge of the language on the census of that year and some of Heuston's acquaintances and colleagues in later life testified to his fluency. But the reason posterity recalls him by the Irish version of his name has more to do with the fact that Heuston fought in the Easter Rising of 1916, and especially with what he told his younger brother, Michael, when he wrote to him on the night of 7 May 1916:

> I suppose you have been wondering why I did not communicate with you since Easter but the explanation is simple. I have been locked up by his Brittanic Majesty's Government. They have just intimated to me that I am to be *executed* in the morning.[1]

Michael Heuston was, at this time, a novice in the Dominican Order, based in Tallaght Priory. His elder brother instructed him that:

> If the rules of the Order allow it I want you to get permission at once and come in here to see me for the last time

in this world. I feel quite prepared to go – thank God, but want you to get all the prayers you can said for me. You will probably be able to come in the motor car which takes out this note.[2]

Presumably he did so, because Michael Heuston, along with Fr Michael – later Cardinal – Browne, then Master of Novices at Tallaght, arrived in Kilmainham Gaol at around 9.40 pm. The guards took their names and after some confusion about Browne's status – the guards were initially unwilling to let in any priests apart from the official chaplains – they were brought in to see the prisoner they had come to visit.[3] Michael Heuston later wrote an account of his visit to Kilmainham and of his last conversation with his older brother. It was intended for their sister Mary, who was a nun in Galway, and it recorded their conversation in exceptional, verbatim detail. It is unusual to have an account like this and we are lucky to have it. Along with the details of the conversation, Michael also recorded the circumstances in which it took place.

Two soldiers – 'with candles' escorted the two clerics 'down a sloping passage into a covered courtyard with the cell' – apparently number thirteen – to his left. Michael Heuston noticed a gas burner located in a hole in the wall; it was not lit. Upon entering the dim cell, 'Jack' – Michael never referred to his older sibling as 'Seán' – 'came forward to meet me. He had an overcoat on but no ordinary coat, and I thought an old, grey waistcoat, but Duckie' – their sister, Teresa – 'says he had his own brown one, though the overcoat was not his own. He had an old, dirty-looking silk-looking handkerchief tied round his neck. He had no collar. He was unshaven, drawn, and dreadfully troubled looking. There was a little blood on his left cheek.'

The cell itself was quite small and inevitably spartan,

about fifteen feet long by six feet broad at the door, widen-ing to nine or ten feet at the end, and about ten feet high. There was a barred window some two feet square high up in the end wall. The walls were whitewashed, the floor was of boards running lengthwise. On the left of the door on entering was a place with tins for food. Then a small, new wooden table with writing materials, and a stool. On the right was a shelf about five feet from the ground, with a crust with the soft part eaten out on it. There was a grey cap on it, but it was not Jack's own. There was nothing in the nature of a bed except a roll of blankets near the table.

The soldiers remained to guard the brothers: one stayed at the door, while the other entered the cell. 'Jack came over to me and shook hands with me. He had his rosary in his hand. He looked at me a fair while before he spoke. He spoke drag-gingly and in a dazed manner.' One of the soldiers assured the brothers that, 'You needn't mind us. We'll make no use of anything you say.' Michael was surprised to find that the soldiers did not insist on their conversation being spoken aloud, as his older brother put an arm around his neck.

'Well, Michael, how are you? Don't cry now,' said Seán. 'So I didn't come out to you on Easter Monday. I thought we would have. We were to have a camp at Rathfarnham, but then this thing came off. Were you able to come all right? I thought it might have been against the rules. Did the motor-car go for you?'

Michael assured Seán that 'there was no difficulty about coming, and that the brothers were saying the Rosary for him.' Their last conversation continued in an almost every-day manner for some time.

'What time did you get the letter?' said Seán.

'About nine o'clock,' was the reply.

'So it must have gone immediately.'

'When did you hear?'

'Just tonight. I got the paper – "confirmed by J.G. Max-well". I wrote to you immediately. I was afraid you might not get it in time, that you might be in bed. I have also written for Mother and Teasie and Duckie'; these latter two were his aunt and sister, both named Teresa. 'I wrote, too, to Mary' – their eldest sister – 'and some others, Mr Walsh, Dalton, Tierney of Limerick.' Seán pointed out the letters on the table to Michael.

'I was writing while waiting for you. Did anyone come with you?'

'Yes, Fr Browne.'

'Where is he? Did he not come in?'

'They would not let him in.'

'What?' Heuston began to remonstrate with one of his guards. 'Would they not let Fr Browne in?'

'Ah, now,' said Michael, 'Don't mind, it's all right I suppose they couldn't. He'll say mass for you in the morning and so will some of the other priests.'

At this point Browne joined the Heustons in the cell, having been delayed by the guards. But, he assured them, 'the corporal was a decent fellow, willing to strain a point.' Seán thanked him for coming and, as Michael Heuston recalled:

> Fr Michael said something to him about meeting him before when visiting me in Tallaght. He said something to him about offering his death as his purgatory and he said he would. Jack asked Fr Michael could he speak alone with him for a few minutes.

But this could pose difficulties:

> Fr Michael was afraid he might want to go to confession to him and that, if he did, the prison authorities might not let the other priests [in] to him later on, saying that he had already been attended to, so he asked him would he not have the other priest later and Jack said it was alright so. Fr Michael had some office to say and he left us alone while he said it.

Browne, in his own words, 'withdrew a little to allow them' – the Heuston brothers – 'to be alone together.'[4] As he did so he heard weeping from the cell next door – number eighteen, in which Michael Mallin of the Irish Citizen Army was imprisoned – and Browne went to offer such consolation as he could to Mallin and his family.

Back in Heuston's cell, the 'soldier who had come into the cell had moved back to the door.'

'Can you stay?' asked Seán.

'I can stay all night if we are let,' replied Michael. 'What time will it be?'

'It' was his brother's impending execution.

'A quarter to four.'

'They are giving you a soldier's death anyhow. It is better than hanging.'

'Yes, they are giving us a soldier's death. I am quite ready to go. I am dying for Ireland. We thought we would have succeeded. Perhaps we won't fail next time. I was at confession and communion at Easter too. The chaplain will bring us communion at half twelve tonight, and Fr Aloysius will come at two o'clock.' 'Fr Aloysius' was the Capuchin Fr Albert; Heuston had confused the names.

'You had mass then today?'

'Yes, but not last Sunday when we were in Arbour Hill.'

'How many are there?'

'There is [Michael] Mallin, a Citizen Army man, and Kent

[Éamonn Ceannt].'

'How did they choose out you?'

'I don't know. We killed a lot of soldiers and two officers. They found Connolly's orders on me, but I think they got something else against me too.'

'You were in the Mendicity Institute,' asked Michael. 'What is it?'

'It's a place over on the South Quays – the quay before Guinness. How did you know I was there?'

'Fr Browne was in looking for you last Tuesday, but could find nothing about you. Mother told him that you were in the Mendicity Institute. On Wednesday we heard you were in prison. Yesterday we heard you were wounded in hospital and Fr Browne was talking with me today of coming in tomorrow to try and see you, as he thought it would be easy for him if you were wounded. Were you wounded at all?'

'No.'

'Someone said she saw you at Stoneybatter on Easter Tuesday. Were you there?'

'No. It must have been someone else she saw.'

'Had you much fighting at the Mendicity Institute?'

'No, not much. We were not there so much to fight as to keep the troops from going down the quay into the city – the Four Courts, etc. We kept them back for two full days. Not one could pass down while we were there …'

The conversation continued for some time, but Heuston

had come to the reason why he now found himself imprisoned. And, just as he had been told earlier that evening, in
the early hours of the next morning, 8 May 1916, Seán Heuston was executed by a British firing squad in the grounds
of Kilmainham Gaol. On 4 May he had been tried by court
martial in Richmond Barracks in Inchicore and was found
guilty of participating in 'an armed rebellion and in the
waging of war against his Majesty the King, such act being
prejudicial to the Defence of the Realm and being committed with the intention and for the purpose of assisting the
enemy.'[5] The United Kingdom of which Ireland was a part
was, after all, at war.

This was the general charge levelled at Heuston. It arose
from his specific activities in the events of the Easter Rising,
as the man in charge of an outpost whose size belied its
significance. The Mendicity Institution was a charity based
on the south quays of the River Liffey that had been providing food and sustenance to the poor of Dublin's inner city
for almost a century. Based in an old townhouse, it had an
importance to the insurgents as it overlooked a natural entry
point into Dublin city centre; as troops began to enter the
city centre, Heuston's small garrison began to exchange fire
with them. The British endured heavy casualties at another
key junction on Dublin's southside – Mount Street Bridge
– but while the fighting around the Mendicity was nowhere
near as bloody as there, the street battle that Heuston and

his men became embroiled in was, in theory, of a similar significance.

Michael Heuston later tried to understand what his brother had got involved in. Some days after Seán's execution – 'the Thursday following' – Michael Heuston went over to the Mendicity Institution, 'but could find no trace of anything except three or four bullet marks on the walls outside and the windows all broken, not by rifle fire, but as it were by the Volunteers themselves.'[6] He returned to the Mendicity the following Tuesday 'and got into it. The people were put out on Easter Monday by the Volunteers. The soldiers they shot down were diagonally across the river at the other side and so were at a considerable distance. They must have been good marksmen to single out the officers and kill them at such a distance', though the precise details remained obscure; 'it is, of course, quite evident that Jack's pistols could not have carried across the river.' Seán Heuston, while talking to his brother, had mused on the various reports and rumours he had heard about the efficiency (or otherwise) of the British troops involved in the fighting across the city, but it would seem that those who had been fighting around the Mendicity had been good at their job.

'The soldiers then surrounded the Institute,' wrote Michael, 'cutting off the means of retreat.' Michael tried to make sense of the scene as he was shown around the building, presumably by a caretaker:

The man who showed me round told me he walked up and down several times and he saw not a single Volunteer at the windows. The soldiers here seem to have been good shots, for I saw few traces on the outside, but the inside was full of holes from the bullets. The direction of the holes showed that shots had come from above and below them on the quays, and I think some even from the other side of the river, possibly from the roofs of the houses, for some few holes were low down – lower even than the window sills. There were two or three holes right through the floor of the first storey into the ground storey. At one place half a door was shot away and a hole about eighteen by nine inches made right through the floor. This was where one of the Volunteers was badly wounded. The man said the place was full of blood here. These were, of course, the work of the grenades. He said to throw these, the soldiers came round quite close under cover of some low walls. When they succeeded in getting them in, the Volunteers held out no time [sic]. One of the Volunteers took a gold pin away. This was found on him at Arbour Hill, I hope this is not true. Some of the soldiers quietly removed £9 or £10 of his. He said, including broken furniture etc, there was about £60 [worth of] damage done.

It would be impossible to recreate Michael Heuston's pilgrimage to survey the aftermath of the fighting today, for the original building is gone (though it is sobering to think that almost a century after Irish independence, the Mendicity Institution continues to feed Dublin's poor from another building on the same site, just as it had done for over a century beforehand). The significance of the Easter Rising to the struggle for independence is unlikely to be disputed; what this short book is concerned with is the figure whose role in the Rising is inextricably linked to the Mendicity Institution. Seán Heuston (to use the most common version of his name) was born in Dublin's inner city slums and was one of the youngest (along with Edward Daly) of those executed in the aftermath of the Rising; a fact that made his execution all the more controversial. Every day Heuston's surname plays a part in thousands of journeys through the train station that bears it. This biography is intended to flesh out the life of an individual who, all too often, is simply listed as one of W.B. Yeats' sixteen dead men.

What can we know of the life he led beforehand?

Chapter 1:

Heuston's Dublin

1891–1911

Seán Heuston was born John Joseph Heuston on 21 February 1891 at 24 Lower Gloucester Street (now Seán MacDermott Street), the son of John Heuston, a clerk, and his wife Maria (née McDonald).[7] John Heuston – Seán's father – was born on 10 August 1865 at 65 Great Strand Street, the son of John Heuston, a porter, and his wife Mary Anne (née Clarke). Heuston's mother, Maria was born on 29 December 1867 at 61 Marlborough Street, the daughter of Michael McDonnell, a bedroom porter, and his wife Mary (née McGrath). The civil authorities seem to have confused the surname of Heuston's mother; even on the birth certificate of her youngest child, Michael, born in 1897, her maiden name was given as 'McDonnell'. But such glitches were not unknown; it seems likely that this was indeed the Maria McDonald who had been baptised in the Pro-Cathedral (also on Marlborough Street) on 31 December 1866 and who married John Heuston in the same venue on 22 January 1888.[8] Seán Heuston's roots lay in Dublin's north inner city.

Of the sixteen men executed after the Easter Rising, six – Heuston, Roger Casement, Michael Mallin, the Pearse brothers and Joseph Mary Plunkett – were from Dublin. With the possible exception of Mallin, Heuston came from the humblest background of them all. His father, John, was a clerk, though the precise details of his job and his background remain obscure, as do many of the details of Heuston's early life. Clerical jobs in the capital were reasonably meritocratic, insofar as the closed shops operating in other professions and trades rarely applied to them. By the end of the nineteenth-century there was a slow but sure increase in the numbers of clerks from working-class backgrounds; a small indicator that social mobility wasn't unheard of in Victorian Dublin. But the key criterion for clerical jobs was an education. This meant that they were effectively restricted to families who could afford to keep a child in education, and this placed them beyond the reach of the vast ranks of the unskilled labouring poor.[9] Heuston's father was lucky in one sense, but the address at which the family lived in 1891 points very strongly towards the world from which they came and from which, presumably, they were trying to escape.

At the time of their marriage Heuston's father lived at 12 North James's Street and his mother at 34 Jervis Street.

They began their family at 24 Gloucester Street, on the fringes of the vast Gardiner estate north of the River Liffey. This had been developed by the Gardiner family from the 1720s onwards and its centrepiece was Sackville Street and Gardiner's Mall, both of which would later be merged into Sackville – O'Connell – Street. The estate was one of the most prestigious residential areas of what was, in the eighteenth-century, a city dominated by the Protestant aristocracy known to history as the 'ascendancy'.[10] Dublin had been a centre of administration, education, the judicial system and trade for centuries; its reworking as a 'Protestant' capital city during the eighteenth-century went hand in hand with an extraordinary growth. Many of its public buildings and much of the streetscape that its inhabitants were still familiar with in the early twentieth-century dated from that era; by *circa* 1800 Dublin's population had tripled within a century to approximately 182,000. Even aside from the presence of the aristocracy (who accounted for a large chunk of the city's economy), eighteenth-century Dublin had become a significant manufacturing centre and a major distribution point for imported goods. Its cultural and political influence was unmatched on the island and the description of Dublin as the apocryphal 'second city' of the British Empire makes a great deal of sense in relation to the eighteenth-century. Yet the same cannot be said of the nineteenth.

Dublin has presented a number of faces to the world, but

two of the best known go hand in hand, as the splendour of the eighteenth century gave way to the squalor of the nineteenth. There were various reasons for this transition, but the symbolic dividing line was usually taken to be the Act of Union of 1800. The formal integration of the Irish parliament with its British counterpart meant that Ireland's ruling elites began to leapfrog Dublin en route to London, and the aristocracy for whom much of the city was remodelled slowly but surely abandoned it. This was not the only reason for Dublin's decline, but it was a very visible mark of it. Take, for example, Aldborough House, located a few hundred yards from Heuston's eventual birthplace in the north of the city. Completed in 1799 for John Stratford, second earl of Aldborough (who died in 1801), it was apparently meant to rival Leinster House on the southern side of the River Liffey, but ironically, was the last aristocratic mansion to be built anywhere in the city. It later became a barracks, which helped to sustain the large and notorious red light district that sprang up in the streets around Heuston's birthplace: 'Monto'.

The Act of Union was indeed a landmark in the history of both Ireland and its capital, with Dublin now becoming a regional capital within the new United Kingdom. Aldborough House may have been the last of its kind, but other building projects continued after 1800 (though not on an eighteenth-century scale): the GPO (1818), King's Inns

(1820), the commissioners for Education on Marlborough Street (1835-61) and the prisons at Arbour Hill (1848) and Mountjoy (1850), to name a few that formed a backdrop to Heuston's life. The city that he grew up in had not come to a shuddering halt at the turn of the nineteenth-century: Dublin continued to grow after the union. But the rate at which it did so was much reduced and the size of its population gives an indication of its decline: in 1891, the year of Heuston's birth, the population was only 245,000. Even aside from the loss of the aristocracy and the parliament, Dublin embarked upon a downward spiral in the decades after 1800, as its traditional industries (such as textile manufacturing) were whittled away. Within the newly-expanded United Kingdom, Dublin's primary function was as a transit point for the export of food and people and the importation of British goods: a perpetual motion driven by the imperatives of Britain's industrial centres. The vast bulk of its trade was with the rest of the UK rather than the rest of the world; the docks that lay so close to Heuston's place of birth were in no way comparable to the great docklands of Britain. Dublin was not an industrial city; other than food processing it lacked labour-intensive industries, and was in no position to compete with other major UK cities like Birmingham, Glasgow, Liverpool or Manchester.

There were, however, some shards of light amidst the gloom. By the end of the nineteenth century Dublin had acquired some important constellations of new buildings: the museums clustered around Leinster House, new churches, the banks that had grown around College Green and the massive commercial edifice of the Guinness brewery. Likewise, by 1891 its infrastructure was much improved, with new water supplies and a new tram network. The railway boom of the later nineteenth century had given Dublin a ring of new stations around its centre (and later gave Seán Heuston a job). But this was all somewhat piecemeal. Dublin did not experience the wholesale rebuilding that characterised many other capital or industrial cities. What it did witness was urban decline and a widening gap between rich and poor in a de-industrialised city. In the mid-nineteenth century, this economic stagnation was accompanied by one of the most significant social developments in the city's history, as the emerging Catholic (and remaining Protestant) middle classes abandoned the city between the canals and relocated to new townships such as Clontarf and Rathmines. In the vacuum left behind, slums and tenements flourished, and this had major implications for many of those who continued to live within the city proper. Dubliners were perhaps the least likely of Irish people to choose emigration, but if poverty and deprivation were reasons to emigrate, than Dubliners had more reason than most.

The poverty that was seen to characterise Dublin by the late nineteenth century was a product of decline. It had long been noted as a feature of urban life, but the problem had got worse after the union, as the eighteenth-century estates declined into slums characterised by disease, disrepair, malnutrition and poor sanitation. Over the nineteenth-century, poverty became a more visible problem as it colonised previously-fashionable areas left behind by both the ascendancy and the middle classes who had followed them, most notably the old Gardiner estate, which witnessed a remarkable collapse in its social composition from the 1850s onwards. Gloucester Street was a perfect example of a street that had declined: as early as 1885 one house on the street had been used as an example of urban squalor for the benefit of a public inquiry and by 1899 some 55 per cent of its houses were either tenements, or were derelict.[11]

The social and economic structure of Dublin did little to soften these blows. The population of the greater Dublin area stood at 404,000 in 1911; an increase from 317,000 in 1851, which was demographically unique in Ireland. But Dublin's patterns of employment were also distinctive. In 1841 as many as 33 per cent of the male workforce was employed in manufacturing; that proportion had come down to 20 per cent by 1911. As the city continued to shed its remaining industries while its population continued to expand, casual and unskilled labour became increasingly important: by 1911 one in five of all male workers in the city could be categorised thus. The poor had to take whatever work they could get and this posed barriers to their advancement: clerical work, for instance, required an education that was beyond the reach of many tenement dwellers, as the necessity for casual employment got in the way. Skilled labour tended to stay within family networks and there was competition for casual labour from immigrants from the countryside. The more secure labouring occupations – policing, government, corporation, brewing, tramways and railways – were dispro-portionately occupied by migrants from elsewhere in Ire-land. In other words, Dublin's poorer classes were squeezed even further into the area of casual, unskilled labour. Given their address in 1891, the Heustons were lucky to have a regular breadwinner, however modest. In a city starved of industry, prospects for improvement became more limited the further down the social scale one was. And Gloucester Street was very far down that scale.

But the family managed to move away from there. By 8 June 1897 – the date of birth of their youngest child, Michael – the Heustons were living at 34 Jervis Street, another slum area in the north inner city.[12] Thirty-two people had been killed by tuberculosis on Gloucester Street between 1894 and 1897: reason enough to move a small family, perhaps, but we cannot be sure.[13] According to the census of April 1901 there were four families in 34 Jervis Street, one of the smaller dwellings on a street with over nine hundred inhabitants. Seán Heuston's family occupied three rooms in what was categorised as both a first-class dwelling and a tenement. There was, however, one notable absentee in 1901: his father. John and Maria Heuston had four children. The eldest was Mary, aged twelve in 1901, followed by John – Seán – aged ten, Teresa, aged eight and Michael, aged three. But John Heuston had left the family home at some point after Michael's birth and it would appear that the family had moved in with Maria's two unmarried sisters: Teresa McDonald, thirty-two, who was recorded as the head of the family and who worked as an envelope maker, and Brigid, thirty, who worked as a vest maker. Between that and the fact that their father was absent, it is possible that they had fallen on hard times and that John Heuston had left his wife and children in search of work. But we cannot be certain.

Like their counterparts in so many times and places, the urban poor of Victorian Dublin left relatively few traces behind them, except insofar as they were noticed by official-dom. The Heuston family is no exception. The reasons why John Heuston left the family home remain unknown, but at the time of his eldest son's death, in May 1916, he was living in London. A letter that Seán wrote to his father on the eve of his execution hinted at an estrangement; it stated that he had not seen his father for many years and had become the main breadwinner for the family. Given his youth, it seems likely that Seán had not seen his father since childhood and, given the circumstances that he wrote of, his father may well have left to seek work elsewhere. Yet the fact that Heuston's mother and father were in a position to contact one another after their eldest son's execution suggests that family affairs were not automatically acrimonious.

At this remove it is impossible to penetrate the inner workings of Seán Heuston's family. But what we can do is take note of the appalling poverty and squalor of the areas in which he was born and raised, and to which he could not have been oblivious. The decayed poverty of places such as Gloucester Street and Jervis Street was evident in photographic evidence presented to the 1913 inquiry into Dublin's tenement problem, undertaken after the collapse of two tenement houses on Church Street in 1913; another place that Heuston would come, in time, to be very familiar with.[14] But by then his family had left Jervis Street as well as Gloucester Street and Heuston no longer resided in the city of his birth.

Chapter 2:

• • • • •

Heuston's Ireland

Heuston was born in 1891: the same year that the Home Rule leader Charles Stewart Parnell died, though the cause Parnell espoused continued to dominate Irish nationalism over the course of Heuston's relatively short life. Heuston died for his involvement in a separatist uprising, but the separatism that he and his colleagues adhered to had been on the fringe of Irish politics in the years after 1891. Indeed, it had been on the fringes for years before then. In 1891 the Irish Republican Brotherhood (IRB), members of which would eventually plan the Easter Rising, remained moribund and ineffectual. In the decades after the failed 'Fenian' rebellion of 1867 separatist republicanism had become marginalised and from the 1870s onwards the demand for Home Rule had the field to itself. It was still what most Irish nationalists were demanding from Britain on the eve of the First World War.

Home Rule meant limited self-government; a form of

devolution. The basic principle was that Ireland would remain a constituent part of the United Kingdom, but a domestic parliament or legislature would be established in Dublin to administer some of its its internal affairs. Home Rule came to real prominence in the 1880s under Parnell's stewardship of the Irish MPs in Westminster; the Liberal Prime Minister William Ewart Gladstone had supported the introduction of a Home Rule Bill before parliament in 1886. But for many in Britain, especially in the ranks of the Conservative Party, Irish Home Rule was a dangerous idea to be opposed. Assuming that the Irish were capable of governing themselves (there was often a racist undertone to that debate), might the sight of Ireland gradually extricating itself from the rule of the imperial parliament set a very dangerous precedent for other parts of the British Empire? Gladstone's party had split over this very issue and Irish Home Rule remained unpopular in Britain: in 1893 a second Home Rule Bill passed the House of Commons, only to be vetoed in the House of Lords. A third Home Rule Bill passed through the House of Commons in 1912, but the veto power of the Lords had been stripped away and its implementation was seen as inevitable.

In other words, for most of Heuston's life the Home Rule movement, despite the disarray it had fallen into after Parnell's acrimonious fall from grace, had retained its grip on the hearts and minds of nationalist Ireland. The reunification of Parnell's party under the relatively moderate leadership of John Redmond gave it a degree of renewed momentum. Given the fact that one of the great British political parties was committed, albeit reluctantly, to the cause of Irish Home Rule, there seemed little reason for Redmond and his followers to fall prey to a rival ideology; all that they required for success was a certain combination of circumstances and they were bound to come with time.

By the beginning of the twentieth century, despite Ireland's social and economic problems and the deep grievances built up by centuries of British rule – at best resented and at worst despised by many Irish nationalists – there was a very real chance that Ireland would be reconciled to an existence within the United Kingdom and the Empire should Home Rule eventually be granted. Though Home Rule politicians were capable of fiery rhetoric that was wholly at odds with the quite limited measure of self-government that they were after, their objective was vague enough to satisfy all kinds of aspirations. But the essential point is this: the political backdrop to Seán Heuston's life was very far from being republican.

There were, however, other backdrops. Towards the end of the nineteenth century, the sense that Ireland was becoming increasingly anglicised prompted an upsurge in 'cultural' nationalism, which took a number of forms. The increasing popularity of games such as soccer, rugby, and cricket (Heuston seemed to favour the latter) prompted the formation of the Gaelic Athletic Association (GAA) in 1884 and the precipitous decline of *Gaeilge,* the indigenous Irish language, had prompted the formation of the Gaelic League (*Conradh na Gaeilge*) in 1893 for the purpose of reviving it. Such cultural nationalism enjoyed support amongst many nationalists, but if its broad thrust was to assert that Ireland was culturally distinct from Britain, then it was only a short step towards asserting that Ireland should also be politically separate. At the same time, an involvement in cultural movements did not automatically go hand in hand with an involvement in political movements. But sometimes, it did. Douglas Hyde, the co-founder of the Gaelic League, had issued his famous call for the 'de-anglicisation' of Ireland in 1893, two years after Heuston's birth. And the 1901 census recorded that Heuston, at the age of ten, was the only member of his family to have a knowledge of Irish as well as English.

Heuston was educated by the Christian Brothers at Great Strand Street and later at their O'Connell Schools on North Richmond Street.[15] This may have contributed to his interest in Irish: the Christian Brothers were the first religious order to teach it in any meaningful way. Their willingness to do so had been evident from the 1870s and they were prominent in the campaign to include Irish on the school curriculum, which had succeeded in 1878. The O'Connell Schools seemed to place a particular emphasis on Irish: in 1901 a group of former pupils established a medal competition for success in the Irish exams, and this interest in the language may have dovetailed with another crucial component of the Christian Brothers' approach that was obvious by the start of the twentieth century: the emphasis on teaching an unequivocally nationalistic version of Irish history.[16] The *Irish History Reader* that the brothers published in 1905 distilled the 'lessons of Irish history' in the following manner: given that once 'dark and evil days dawned on Ireland' in which 'ruthless persecution burst upon the land and strove by rack and fire and sword to kill the faith which Patrick brought to your ancestors', it was incumbent on their charges to remain fast to that faith. But they were not merely to look to the past: they were to apply its lessons to the future. 'In a few short years, you will go forth to take your place amongst men; recall, then, this sad fact of the past and learn from it, that if you are to help the cause of Faith and Fatherland, you must avoid dissension and shun all that might tend to create disunion.' Furthermore, the students were implored to 'be temperate' and to 'live your life in Ireland'. Finally, 'as men, have a share in every movement that make for the upraising and well-being of your country'; to do so was to 'discharge a sacred duty'.[17]

It is tempting to work back from here to speculate about what Heuston thought of all this. After his execution, his mother gave an interview in which she expressed strongly nationalist sentiments, and was scornful of the Home Rulers; her children may well have been brought up in a strongly nationalist household.[18] But we cannot be certain. What we can say without any equivocation is that Seán Heuston was a successful student: he sat his intermediate exams in 1905 and won a book prize worth £3. The following year he won a prize worth £10, having received honours marks in a number of subjects, including Irish, English, French, algebra, arithmetic and science. He scored high grades in 1907 during his middle grade year, with honours in English, Irish, Algebra, Trigonometry and Science.[19] By this time the Heuston family were living at 50 Dominick Street (another tenement area), though the 1911 census revealed that their father was still absent.[20] Seán may have worked for Joseph Kennedy, a tailor with premises at 44 Lower Ormond Quay, though this is unclear.[21] But his family needed a breadwinner and Heuston had put Kennedy down as a reference for the job he applied for in the summer of 1907: as a clerk in the Great Southern & Western Railway (GSWR).[22]

Railways were one of the major industrial success stories of nineteenth-century Ireland. Perhaps seventy-five companies operated in Ireland between 1834 and 1900 and the GSWR was one of the largest from the outset. It had been founded by the London & Birmingham Railway and was incorporated by an Act of Parliament in August 1844, opening its first line, from Dublin to Carlow, two years later.[23] It swallowed up a number of smaller companies in the course of its growth, as the Irish railways underwent a massive expansion in the nineteenth century: sixty-five miles of track in 1845 had become 3,500 by 1914. Irish railways were less profitable than their British counterparts as they did not serve heavy industry to the same extent, but this was offset by the fact that railway construction was much cheaper in Ireland thanks to lower infrastructure and labour costs.[24] By the end of the nineteenth century the GSWR was responsible for a third of the Irish network, with 1,150 miles of track linking Dublin, Cork and Limerick, and the largest depot in Ireland at Kingsbridge station near Inchicore.[25]

But the rail companies were products of their time in other ways. The business and governmental elites of Edwardian Ireland were disproportionately Protestant and unionist in composition; the GSWR was no exception (it had paid a bonus to all staff for maintaining its services during the Fenian Rising of 1867). In 1902 and 1903 the Catholic polemicist D.P. Moran, in his capacity as editor of the nationalist newspaper *The Leader*, published a number of articles alleging that the three main railway companies (the GSWR, the Great Northern, and the Midland Great Western) used sectarian reruitment policies. In particular, the GSWR (or, as Moran put it, 'the Great Sourface Railway') was singled out for its alleged discrimination against Catholic workers.[26] In February 1903 the company announced that in order to dispel suggestions of 'undue preference', clerkships were to be opened to the public and examinations for posts would hitherto be competitive, with two examiners: one Protestant and one Catholic. Candidates had to know one foreign language: French, German or Latin. Irish was not yet deemed admissible, lest it seem 'sentimental', despite the fact that the GSWR network traversed some of the remaining *Gaeltachtaí*.[27] It was not until March 1907 that Irish was included in the clerkship examinations. Heuston was part of the first batch to have the opportunity to be examined in this way and he opted to take the language tests in both French and Irish. It is striking that of the 136 applicants who took the examinations with him, fifty-one had opted to be examined in Irish; an indication of the priorities of at least some members of what Fearghal McGarry has dubbed 'the rising generation'.[28]

Heuston's application for a clerkship in the GSWR was received on 21 June 1907. Clerkships were always in demand and attracted huge numbers of applicants. The reasons why were easy to understand: they were well paid when compared to manual labour (with an eight-hour day to boot). The relatively low rates of rail traffic made for a fairly leisurely workplace and the dismissal rates for indoor staff were quite low (outdoor staff tended to get fired for drunkenness), though the actual clerkship exam was quite rigorous.[29] Candidates had to pay a ten shilling fee, were then interviewed, took the exams and finally had to pass a medical examination. Heuston and his fellow candidates were examined at the Royal University Buildings (now the National Concert Hall) on Earlsfort Terrace, just off Stephen's Green, on 16 July 1907. They were questioned on their knowledge of languages, geography, English composition, algebra and arithmetic. Heuston came fifth out of 136 applicants, only twenty-five of whom were successful. The subsequent medical examination on 1 August concluded that Heuston was 'free from any disease tending to shorten life, or from any physical defect likely to interfere with the proper discharge of his duties'; his eyesight was confirmed as 'good', and on the same day he signed the company's 'declaration of fidelity and secrecy'.[30] Consequently, on 19 August 1907 he was appointed as a probationary clerk at the GSWR depot in Limerick.

Limerick, like Dublin, was another Irish city that had witnessed both Georgian growth and pockets of Victorian decline. The rail network had first reached Limerick in 1848 and Heuston's probationary period there lasted approximately one year. According to his immediate superior, who recommended his permanent appointment on 12 September 1908, Heuston was 'strictly honest', 'strictly sober' and 'of good habits generally'. Furthermore, he was 'punctual', his conduct and the performance of his duties had been 'satisfactory in all respects', he was 'intelligent', 'industrious', in good health, with a 'slight' knowledge of shorthand and a fuller knowledge of book-keeping. He had been employed in 'goods servicing & abstracting and furnishing traders [accounts]'. Finally, when it came to the key question – 'does he promise to become a useful clerk?' – the answer was 'yes, he is particularly satisfactory'.[31] He received a mark of 86 per cent in the examinations for clerkships in the goods department, so in Limerick he would remain.[32]

On the night of the 1911 census twenty people occupied six rooms at 50 Dominick Street in Dublin: the Heuston family occupied two of those rooms.[33] Maria and her children had moved from Jervis Street and her sister, Teresa, now an overseer in an envelope works, had accompanied them. The eldest child, Mary Anne, was a national school teacher and an undergraduate at the National University. Seán, on the other hand, was lodging with Francis Joseph Humphries, a sorting clerk and telegrapher (presumably in the post office), his wife Agnes and their five-year-old son William, at 7 Military Road, Limerick. It was in Limerick that Heuston became involved in the kind of overtly-nationalistic organisations that his employers were unlikely to have approved of.

Chapter 3:

Heuston and Na Fianna

One of the last things that Heuston communicated to his confessor, the Capuchin Father Albert, prior to his execution was the imprecation to 'remember me to the boys of the Fianna.'[34] It was understandable: the organisation that Heuston had been most heavily involved in and with which he was most commonly associated was Na Fianna Éireann, the republican boy scouts founded in Dublin by Bulmer Hobson and Constance Markievicz in August 1909.[35]

Hobson was born in Belfast into a Quaker family. He had helped to found the Fianna as an Irish nationalist alternative to the imperialist ethos of Robert Baden-Powell's Boy Scouts, who had become increasingly active in Ireland since their foundation in 1908 (Baden Powell sought to persuade Patrick Pearse to set up an Irish branch, with a predictably negative result).[36] Hobson tried to establish a youth organisation of the same name in Belfast in 1902, though this foundered due to its lack of resources and Hobson's other commitments. But both the name and Hobson's assistance were appropriated by Markievicz in 1909. Constance Markievicz, neé Gore-Booth, remains one of the more exotic figures of the Irish Revolution: a scion of the Anglo-Irish gentry of Sligo who married a Polish count and became a convert to socialism and Irish republicanism. Markievicz was alarmed that organisations like the Boys' Brigades and Boy Scouts seemed to be attracting the favour of the authorities; consequently, she began to seek support for the foundation of a similar organisation for young nationalists. Tom Clarke provided some advice on whom she might approach and after an abortive attempt at setting up her own organisation (originally dubbed the 'Red Branch Knights') with the assistance, amongst others, of the republican feminist Helena Moloney and William O'Neill (a teacher in St Andrew's National School on Brunswick Street, some of whose students joined the Fianna), she eventually came into contact with Hobson. She was particularly taken with his efforts from 1902 and the two formed an effective combination. Markievicz provided money and a veneer of respectability (though tensions that arose from the involvement of a woman in a movement for boys were never fully dispelled, despite her role in founding it); alongside her, Hobson took care of the nuts and bolts of the organisation.

The first meeting of what became Na Fianna Éireann took place at 34 Camden Street on 16 August 1909. It was attended by between thirty and a hundred boys, all from the south inner city ('adventurers', as one of those present later recalled).[37] Its growth was relatively slow, for various reasons, but by 1916 it had a presence in at least nineteen counties and in émigré communities in Glasgow and Liverpool. The Fianna was established as a youth organisation for boys aged between eight and eighteen. It was to be non-political and adopted a heirarchical structure, with the *Ard-choisde* (central council) at the top and the *Sluagh* ('troop': the plural was *Sluaighte*) acting as the rank and file; the annual *Ard-fheis* (congress) allowed the organisation to meet and co-ordinate as a whole. It sustained itself from membership contributions, fundraising events and occasional donations. In itself, this was not especially unusual, but the Fianna was groundbreaking in one key regard: it was the most openly militaristic nationalist organisation to emerge in Ireland for decades and its emphasis on drilling, fieldcraft and the use of weapons provided a grounding in such activities for members of the IRB and later, the Irish Volunteers. Arguably, it helped to set the stage for what these organisations eventually did, but there was nothing uniquely Irish about the manner in which the Fianna did so.

Na Fianna Éireann was one of innumerable groups of this kind to emerge across Europe in the years prior to the Great War. Organised politics across much of the continent from the second half of the nineteenth-century onwards had often been conducted in a manner infused with the rhetoric of manhood and masculinity, most obviously in terms of espousing and encouraging martial values, or of glorifying heroic actions and deeds.[38] A nation or a homeland might have to be fought for and that fighting was to be done by its men; and what were men once, if not boys?

There was no shortage of militarism in Ireland in the years before 1914 and the Fianna were part of the trend.[39] Its official handbook gave a very strong sense of its ethos (and Heuston was later rumoured to have had 'a good share in the work' of publishing it.)[40] The introduction by Markievicz pulled no punches by stating that the purpose of the Fianna – 'a glorious brotherhood of youth' – was to 'win Independence and Freedom for their country'.[41] A touch of martyrdom was evident too:

> It will take the best and noblest of Ireland's children to win Freedom, for the price of Freedom is suffering and pain. It is only when the suffering is deep enough and the pain almost beyond bearing that Freedom is won. Through the long black record of England's tyranny and oppression, empire building and robbery, many names stand out of noble souls whose lives were given in a passionate protest against their country's wrongs.[42]

Such figures included Joan of Arc, the Manchester Martyrs and the 'many nameless heroes' who 'lie on the South African Veldt'; the Boer War continued to resonate amongst the ranks of militant nationalists:

> The path of freedom may lead us to the same road that Robert Emmet and Wolfe Tone trod. Treading in their footsteps, we will not fear, working as they worked we will not tire and if we must die as they died we will not flinch … Ireland wants you, Ireland is calling you. Join na Fianna Éireann, the young army of Ireland and help to place the crown of freedom on her head. [43]

The declaration to be taken by those who joined it was 'I promise to work for the independence of Ireland, never to join England's armed forces and to obey my superior officers.'[44] As for how a member should conduct himself, he

> must never do anything that would bring discredit upon Ireland or upon the Fianna. He must make himself strong in mind as well as in body. He must learn all about Ireland. He must know her history and learn her language and work to further her interests. He should study and think for himself and be self-reliant and strong. In addition he will receive a military training and he should strive to become so proficient that when Ireland needs soldiers he can take an important place in the fighting line.[45]

Inevitably, the handbook also had instructions on the use of rifles and bayonets and notable contributions on 'chivalry' (by

Roger Casement[46]) and 'The Fianna of Fionn' (by Pearse[47]).
The Fianna constitution, as amended in 1913, stated that the
object of the organisation was 'to reestablish the independence of Ireland' and the means by which it would so was by
'the training of the youth of Ireland, mentally and physically,
to achieve this object by teaching scouting and military exer-
cises, Irish history and the Irish language.'[48] As Bulmer Hobson's monthly paper *Irish Freedom* noted, 'it was to combat
the demoralising influence of the English schools and boys
organisations that "Na Fianna Éireann" was founded'.[49] And
as *Irish Freedom* stated a few months later, in February 1913,
'our aim is not merely to make the boys of Ireland first-
class scouts, but to make them first-class Irish nationalists.'[50]
Given that *Irish Freedom* was effectively a mouthpiece for the
IRB, presumably the brotherhood approved of the organisation too. The IRB had a presence within the Fianna from
the outset: at least three members of its original committee
(Hobson, Patrick McCartan and Seán McGarry) were members and Hobson founded a Fianna circle of the IRB in 1912;
he later claimed that Heuston was one of them.

The Fianna had been established in Limerick as early as
September 1911. Heuston, then aged twenty, was involved in
it from the outset.[51] Even aside from its politics, the organisation may have had other attractions for him. When taking his
clerkship exam in 1907, Heuston had written a composition
on 'sports and pastimes', in which he observed that 'there are

very few, who, at one time or another, do not seek to divert their minds from the weightier affairs of life, by abandoning themselves to the relaxing force of a game of football, cricket, cards, a cycle ride, a country walk, or one of the many other indoor and outdoor games'; and alongside the relaxation of the mind, there was the added virtue of 'the development of the body. Outdoor sports of all kinds bestow some benefit to their followers, [and] make them healthy and more capable of performing their various daily occupations.' He was especially alert to the virtues of cricket, with its emphasis on precision, and 'although a stroke of a cricket ball may cause a hurt, yet the pleasure is worth the risk, and no sport can be wholly devoid of danger.' So, he concluded,

> sports and pastimes of all kinds should be encouraged, especially among the young, because they are thus taught to 'play the game of life' and act in a sportsmanlike way towards their fellow men. They are also physically prepared to journey over the thorny path of life, without prematurely falling by the wayside.[52]

If this was any indication of Heuston's views on physical exercise and an outdoor lifestyle, than an organisation like the Fianna, with its emphasis on fieldcraft and its dedication to 'the training of the youth of Ireland, mentally and physically', was surely going to appeal to him.

Heuston became prominent in the Limerick Fianna

relatively quickly: he represented the '1st City of Limerick Company' at the third Fianna *Ard-fheis* in Dublin's Mansion House as early as 14 July 1912.[53] Edward Daly's sister, Madge, who got to know Heuston during his sojourn in Limerick, recalled him as 'a quiet, unassuming boy' with

> a mature, clear-thinking mind, educated to an excep-
> tional degree in subjects relating to his country. He had an
> extraordinary memory, and could quote day and date for
> most important events in our history. With all he was most
> practical, and had the special quality for managing boys and
> getting the best from them. A fluent Irish speaker, Seán used
> his own language whenever possible.[54]

Heuston's interest in Irish was obvious from the manner in which he signed his name on his schoolbooks (not to mention the 1911 census). He may well have had a burgeon-ing interest in political nationalism from a relatively early age, but his involvement in the IRB and the Fianna took any such interest to another level. According to Madge Daly, Heuston was

> methodical, and planned each year's Fianna programme in
> advance, arranging classes, lectures, marches and examina-
> tions for the boys, and persuading his friends to present
> prizes. He realised that the success of the Fianna movement
> depended on keeping the boys fully occupied and inter-
> ested, and in that work he had the willing help of many

adults … Seán himself took charge of drill, signalling and
general scout training. He spent all of his spare time with
the boys, inspiring them with his lofty ideas.[55]

Heuston's assiduousness was presumably one of the reasons why the Fianna in Limerick were so active, with perhaps 210 members by May 1912 (at least according to the
RIC, who viewed Limerick as perhaps the only significant
centre of Fianna activity in the country).[56] The Limerick
Sluagh 'even opened the first purpose-built official Fianna
Hall in the country, in December 1912.'[57] The veteran Limerick Fenian John Daly (Edward and Madge Daly's uncle)
put some money towards its construction; his presence was
suggestive, as Daly was central to the city's radical nationalist
politics.

Daly was born in Limerick and had fled to the United
States after the failed Fenian uprising of 1867. He returned
in 1869 and remained a lifelong militant, being opposed to
the 'New Departure' of the 1870s. In 1884 he was imprisoned after being caught in possession of explosives in Wol-
verhampton; he served some of his life sentence alongside
Tom Clarke, who was imprisoned for a similar offence.
Daly's case became something of a cause celebré after it was
alleged he had been framed; he was elected MP for Limerick
while still in jail and the case for clemency was vociferously
supported by the young John Redmond, amongst others.
On his release in 1896 Daly opened a bakery in Limerick

(which was apparently the only shop in Ireland to use Irish lettering on its sign) and served as mayor of Limerick, but his undimmed militancy and hostility to the Home Rule party cost him support after he denounced them in the US in 1901 while advocating another rebellion. In 1911 he helped to establish a 'Wolfe Tone Club' in Limerick; ostensibly a debating society, but in reality a front for the IRB. Heuston was apparently one of its earliest members.[58] If so, he was a member of the IRB at the age of twenty.

Heuston himself remains obscure throughout much of this period, but one can get a very clear sense of the world within which he was active outside of working hours, along with a flavour of the attitudes that flourished within it. On 8 December, Daly (whose life story was being serialised in *Irish Freedom* at this time) unfurled the company flag of the Limerick *sluagh* – 'in the name of Na Fianna Éireann and in the name of Ireland' – which, since its foundation about twelve months previously, was apparently the largest in Ireland. They paraded on Little Barrington Street, where the new hall was located, with an accompanying pipe band playing numbers such as 'A Nation Once Again'. On the following Friday, 13 December, the hall was officially opened; Daly, having helped with its construction, seemed to act as an unofficial patron and presided over the ceremony, telling those assembled how

that night it was a lecture hall; after the lecture it would be a classroom, a drill room and a gymnasium. The boys would be taught their own mother tongue, they would be taught the history of their country and would have as their companions night after night the men who knew what freedom was worth and would not barter it – not only [sic] with their lives.

It was officially opened by Bulmer Hobson, in militant mood, and *Irish Freedom* carried a report of his speech. Having expressed his pleasure at the opportunity to address the Fianna,

He [Hobson] then went on to deal with the history of the Fianna movement, and said that, owing to the English conquest, the Irish children, instead of being brought up as independent citizens of Ireland, had been brought up in a condition that would never lead them to the position of bringing independence to their country. They had started that organisation for the purpose of training the boys to be citizens of the Irish nation, for the purpose of teaching the boys that they had a country to love and be proud of, so they might serve that country. The best and brightest traditions of Irish nationalism would be set before them.[59]

Hobson did not stop there. He continued in similar vein, pointing out that the Irish nation that he spoke of had survived against the odds:

England's aim for 740 years was to root the Irish people out of their own country, so that Ireland might be colonised and used for the profit of England. They started first by war, then they began to put the people out of their land, and then followed the educational system by which it was England's intention not to educate the children as Irish, but to make them English. That educational system had denationalised the country, and had done a good deal to kill the Irish language. But, he asked, was the English conquest nearer completion? No. The national spirit was not exhausted, for the people were building up organisations like the one he was addressing, which would bring back the national spirit and keep it alive.[60]

But Heuston seems to have been involved in more than just the organisation that Hobson was addressing. At around this time, he sounded out Patrick Whelan (a future member of the IRA in Limerick) about joining the brotherhood; Whelan was sworn into the same circle as Heuston, where he was amazed to find that the IRB 'head centre' for Limerick City was his own father.[61] The intersections between the various organisations on the radical fringe of Irish nationalism were publicly illustrated a few months later, when John Daly himself addressed the Limerick Fianna in June. The occasion arose from a well-attended series of 'physical culture competitions', hosted by the First City of Limerick Company. The prize giving, on Sunday 11 June, was opened with a rendition of 'The Dead Who Died for Ireland', with the prizes being medals and 'several copies of Mitchel's *Jail Journal* and Standish O'Grady's *Gates of the North*' Daly took the chair to applause and congratulated the winners. Then he addressed them, as a link to a previous generation.

The tenor of his speech to the Limerick Fianna showed that he had hardly mellowed with age. *Irish Freedom* reported it thus:

> In 1863 [sic] his comrades and he [Daly] believed that they were about to go into a fight which would leave the present generation the inheritance of a free Ireland. They had not succeeded in attaining their ideals, and many had paid the penalty of not succeeding, but, thank God, the country was not completely conquered yet. He well remembered the days of his boyhood, and knew that it was not always pleasant to spend the evening hours after school in study, but he appealed to the Fianna of Limerick not to rest content with success in physical culture exercises. He asked them to remember the mind must be trained as well, and urged them to endeavour to acquire a thorough knowledge of the history of Ireland, for unless they know the story of their country they could never love her as they ought. Every member of the Fianna should also strive to obtain a good knowledge of the Irish language. What difference, he asked, was there between the majority of Irish people and their tyrannical oppressors? He feared that, judging by the language they spoke, there was none, for by their

tongues they were all English. The older generation had found their country crushed to the earth beneath the iron heel of England and had little or no opportunity of learning their native language, but the young men of today had opportunities in plenty and should avail of them.

When Ireland spoke Irish the days of the British Government's term in this country would be numbered. In the meantime it was their duty to assert their right to the ownership of their own country and to protest by every practical means against foreign usurpation. He had protested, and English brutality had paralysed his limbs, but England had failed to paralyse his mind or heart, and he still defied her. There was trouble in the air, the nations of Europe were moving rapidly for a crash, and when the crash came he would like to see the grip of Germany on England's throat. Concluding, the speaker again congratulated the Fianna, and expressed the hope that when they assembled to hear the results of the coming years work in physical culture he would have even stronger reason to congratulate them.

His speech was then applauded.[62]

Throughout these years Heuston's star was rising. Soon after the hall was opened, he and some others had been obliged to explain themselves to a local priest who had condemned the Fianna; the priest clarified that his objection was not to the organisation in itself, but to the distractions it provided on Sundays when young boys should have been serving mass and he requested that Heuston and his colleagues 'put that matter right'.[63] At the fourth Fianna *Ard-fheis*, held in the Mansion House on 13 July 1913, Heuston was one of the Limerick Fianna's representatives again. On this occasion, both he and Con Colbert (whom in later years he was often associated with) were elected to the *Ard-choisde*.[64] Heuston attended an *Ard-choisde* meeting on D'Olier Street in Dublin on 30 November 1912; *Irish Freedom*'s report referred to him as 'Seán Mac Aodha', which might suggest a renewed commitment to the language, or a sense that he should set an example to those Fianna boys who were obliged to try and learn it (though this Irish version of his surname was questionable).[65] After all, on this occasion Heuston was one of four (the Fianna organiser and eventual 1916 veteran Liam Mellows was another) appointed to a board to 'examine the Fianna throughout Ireland in the Fianna test'. The board members would confirm the results of the local exams to ensure 'a uniform standard throughout Ireland'.

The test for members required recruits to be familiar (after three weeks) with the objectives of the organisation; to have some knowledge of drill, semaphore and Irish; and finally, to have the money for the uniform, the badge of which was emblazoned with a sunburst and a pike. The three subsequent tests for the members emphasised drilling, first aid, signalling, map reading and compass work, a knowledge of topography, knots, how to light a fire and pitch a tent, tracking, swimming and lifesaving. Members also had to have a knowledge of Irish and of history. The periods chosen for study suggested an emphasis on struggles for independence: as well as studying the history of Ireland from St Patrick to 1782 (along with the Cú Chulainn and Ossianic cycles), members also had to be familiar with the period from 'Grattan's Parliament' to the rebellion of Robert Emmet (1782–1803) and afterwards, with Irish history to 1870: just after the Fenian rising of 1867. [66] There could be little doubt about the tenor of what Heuston had become involved in and according to Liam Mellows, the energetic Heuston did 'herculean work in bringing the organisation to a high state of perfection' in Limerick.[67] Heuston may have become synonymous with the Fianna whilst in Limerick, but his involvement in the organisation would continue after his return to Dublin in 1913.

Chapter 4:

Heuston's Dublin

1913-1916

Heuston came back to Dublin in the autumn of 1913: as of 29 September 1913, he had been appointed to the goods office at the massive GSWR depot at Kingsbridge and on 14 January 1914 was appointed to the traffic manager's office.[68]

These dates correspond with the the height of the Dublin Lockout of 1913. As a clerk working for Ireland's largest rail company, Heuston was in a reasonably secure position; he was unlikely to have been affected in a material sense and left no indication as to what his views on the Lockout were. However, his actions suggest that he was, like so many of his generation, profoundly affected by the great political question of the day: the stand-off between nationalism and unionism that had been prompted by the Home Rule Bill of 1912. This had triggered the renewed militarisation of Irish nationalism and in doing so, gave a boost to those groups on its radical fringes.

As members of the IRB, Heuston and Con Colbert were apparently involved in surreptitiously training younger members of the brotherhood at the Irish National Foresters Hall at 41 Parnell Square, which had been a base for IRB circles for some time.[69] This may have been taking place even before the foundation of the UVF (at which time Heuston was based in Limerick), but it certainly continued afterwards. When the Irish Volunteers were eventually founded in November 1913, senior members of the Fianna, such as Heuston and Colbert, received commissions in the new organisation and helped to train its members.[70] The militarism of the Fianna ensured that its members had expertise to share. That the Fianna were becoming increasingly militant was made evident in February 1914, with the publication in *Irish Freedom* of a manifesto addressed to 'The boys of Ireland'. This stated that

we believe, as every Irish boy whose heart has not been corrupted by foreign influence must believe, that our country ought to be free. We do not see why Ireland should allow England to govern her, either through Englishmen, as at present, or through Irishmen under an appearance of self-government. We believe that England has no business in this country at all ... it is the duty of Irishmen to struggle always, never giving in or growing weary, until they have won back their country.

It then moved from the general to the specific:

The object of Na Fianna Éireann is to train the boys of Ireland to fight Ireland's battle when they are men ... the brave Irish who rose in '98, in '48 and in '67, went down because they were not soldiers: we hope to train Irish boys from their earliest years to be soldiers ...

Imbued not just with military training, but also a 'military spirit', which the Fianna took credit for keeping alive in more recent times; 'if the Fianna had not been founded in 1909, the Volunteers of 1913 would never have arisen.' And if the Fianna were indeed 'the pioneers of the Volunteers', then 'it is from the ranks of the Fianna that the Volunteers must be recruited'.[71] This was a prescient observation, as many, including Heuston himself, would graduate from the ranks of the Fianna into the Volunteers. The manifesto offered a clue to the importance of the history lessons that the Fianna had come to insist upon, for it firmly and unequivocally brought the organisation into the militant separatist tradition.

After returning to Dublin, Heuston was attached to a Fianna *Sluagh* that met in Hardwicke Street, in the north inner city; its members were apparently relieved to find that he was a genial Dubliner with a 'bright and lovable disposition', rather than the 'slow easy going (raw) fellow from the country' that they had feared.[72] Heuston soon impressed them.

He [Heuston] was systematic, lucid and exact in every sphere of military training – sparing no effort, and least of all, no time in drilling and instructing us in the arts of the soldier's trade. His knowledge of the various military subjects surprised us not a little. Where and how he acquired this were questions which many of us asked. It took time, however, to find out that he was a keen student of military training craft and technique extending over a number of years, especially during his stay in Limerick where he was associated with the Fianna company, and he possessed many books, manuals etc on various military matters. In course of time we benefited, our *Sluagh* and the Fianna in general, by that expert knowledge in many ways, and not the least by Seán conducting officers and NCO classes and specialised training of which he showed himself to be a keen and enthusiastic advocate.[73]

Soon after he joined them Heuston's detachment obtained a 'trek-cart': a simple, two-wheeled collapsible cart that could be used to transport their equipment and which was supposedly his brainchild.[74] It came in especially useful on 26 July 1914, when a selection of senior members of the Fianna were mobilised in the hall on Hardwicke Street to participate in the Howth gun running.

The importation of weapons by both the UVF, and to a lesser degree by their counterparts in the Irish Volunteers, offered concrete proof of the militarisation of Irish politics prior to the First World War. The Fianna under Heuston did not know that this is what they were getting involved in when they assembled on the morning of 26 July. Seán Prendergast recalled that their trek cart was quite heavily laden, but that Heuston told them it contained 'only minerals' and that they were 'going on a march to Lucan'. The route they took – across Mountjoy Square, to Jones' Road and down to Ballybough and finally to Father Mathew Park, where members of the Volunteers had assembled – did not arouse any suspicions until it became obvious that they were definitely heading away from the city. They travelled along the Howth Road, through Raheny and, after a rest at Kilbarrack, continued towards Sutton and the Howth peninsula.[75] Upon reaching Howth train station, the Fianna were moved to the head of the column.[76]

At Howth harbour, Prendergast saw Heuston in 'deep and earnest conversation with Bulmer Hobson', before he instructed both him and Patrick Holohan to run down the pier and blow their bugles if they saw a white yacht: the *Asgard*, owned by the Anglo-Irish military veteran Erskine Childers. The yacht was already berthed at the lighthouse on the eastern pier of the harbour. Joseph Lawless recalled that 'as we turned on to the pier I noticed some Volunteer and Fianna officers, including Seán Heuston, standing there and apparently surrounding one or two RIC men who appeared to be intimidated by the display of superior force.'[77] The Volunteers rushed down the pier, but the Fianna were given the task of actually unloading the *Asgard*'s cargo. Heuston and a number of others jumped aboard and 'almost at once, long rifles with gleaming barrels began to appear from the hold and were passed from hand to hand to the waiting men on the pier.'[78] These were the famous 'Howth Mausers'; antiquated but accurate single-shot rifles obtained in Germany. Fianna members formed a human chain and began to pass the guns along the pier, as Heuston instructed another group to load the hand cart with ammunition boxes that were also being unloaded.[79] The cart that Heuston's troop had brought with them was by now emptied of its original contents, which were not 'minerals' of any sort: it had actually been used to transport 'huge truncheons', which were now in the hands of Volunteers lining the approach to the pier as both they and the Fianna began to make their way back to the city; they were to have been used on the police had they tried to interfere.[80]

The Volunteers and Fianna were left unmolested by the authorities until they reached Fairview, where they were confronted by the Dublin Metropolitan Police (DMP) (some of whom were apparently sympathetic to the gun-running) and the King's Own Scottish Borderers, who later shot dead three people on Bachelor's Walk as they returned to the Royal Barracks that afternoon. Rather then enter into an obviously tense situation, Heuston retreated with the Fianna and their cart towards Donnycarney, where they hid the weapons and ammunition. He later arranged for a lorry from Thompsons' Garage, owned by the family of Liam Tobin, to retrieve the cart; Heuston and a number of others retrieved the rifles that had been hidden.[81] Heuston was also alleged to have been involved in the related, but far less public, landing of weapons at Kilcoole in County Wicklow at the beginning of August. The weapons in question were the remainder of the Mauser rifles purchased in Germany; presumably the Volunteers had learnt from what happened at Howth, as the Kilcoole guns were landed at night (from a yacht belonging to Sir Thomas Myles, the chief medical officer of the Richmond Hospital) and to avoid the unwanted attention of the authorities, the RIC in Bray were held captive at gunpoint. But Heuston's role in these events, if any, remains unclear.[82]

Heuston kept his *Sluagh* active throughout the summer and the autumn of 1914, leading them on excursions to Castlebar and Courtown, sometimes as guests of local detachments of the Fianna.[83] He was 'particularly keen on night manoeuvres, route marches and street fighting', and instructed his troop accordingly; at one point he also put a group of the Fianna though intensely–detailed preparations to compete in a drill and training competition for the Volunteers held at St Enda's.[84] (He, Colbert and Liam Mellows also apparently helped to train the students of St Enda's, at the request of Patrick Pearse.[85]) The Fianna were, by now, becoming even more militant and Heuston played a role in this too. At one procession that assembled at St Stephen's Green in order to march to Glasnevin, Heuston's troop was disgruntled to find that some other units of the Fianna were armed and demanded the same treatment.

'All right,' said Heuston. 'We shall see what can be done.'

He led his small detachment to the Fianna Hall on Camden Street (where the organisation had originally been founded), 'where to our greater surprise', recalled Prendergast, 'we were issued with a number of rifles': .22 caliber Springfield rifles that had been smuggled into Ireland from the United States. The Howth rifles had been earmarked for the Irish Volunteers; these American weapons were a new development and the Fianna subsequently brought them on their march. This was the first time that Prendergast and his Fianna colleagues had carried weapons in public and as far as he was concerned, 'the presence and possession of these rifles put the Fianna on a new footing. No more broom handles, no more dummy rifles … we were an "army" now.'[86]

After the outbreak of the First World War in August 1914, the Irish Volunteers had split over whether or not to follow John Redmond's call to support the war effort. The vast majority did, but a minority did not. Those who did follow Redmond were re-named the 'National Volunteers'. Despite breaking away from the main body of the Volunteer movement, the smaller faction managed to hold on to the original name and after the split, Heuston became increasingly active in the Irish Volunteers, having previously represented the Fianna on the Volunteer executive. [87] He now had 'a double role to play in forwarding the interests of both forces', and soon Heuston was even instructing the Fianna to gather information on British troops and what Prendergast called 'the other side'; the 'Redmondite' National Volunteers.[88] At Easter 1915, on the same weekend that Redmond's Volunteers held a major review in the Phoenix Park, Heuston and Colbert led members of the Irish Volunteers on a gruelling overnight march (described by one participant as a 'forced march') from Rathfarnham to Rathdrum, Glencree, Roundwood and back to Dublin. They were finally dismissed at the Parnell monument on O'Connell Street, having walked 'almost eighty miles in less than forty-eight hours.'[89] The members of this 'agony column' had marched in full kit (though without rifles); forty-three out of fifty completed it.[90]

It should be pointed out that these activities were taking place during the First World War. Ireland, as part of the United Kingdom, had gone to war in August 1914 and this was the essential backdrop against which the Easter Rising took place: it gave the IRB their opportunity. There was a good deal of pro-war (and anti-German) sentiment to be found in Ireland and in Dublin, assiduously fostered by Redmondite support for the war effort and, in practical terms, prompted by existing traditions of Irish service in the British armed forces: the army offered a path out of poverty that many Dubliners were prepared to take. Indeed, Heuston's employers in the GSWR followed their unionist instincts by offering bonuses to employees who enlisted and benefits for their families (though they were obliged to juggle this with maintaining their staff levels). By 1915 the company was distributing enlistment forms to all of its employees; presumably Heuston declined the offer.[91] By the end of the year, however, enthusiasm for the war was waning as its human and material cots impinged upon life in the city.[92] But the war did have an incidental usefulness for the British authorities in Ireland: the reconfiguration of Irish political life after its outbreak made it much easier to identify more radical nationalists, given that they had opposed the war from the outset. And the ongoing conflict was a further reason to keep a close watch on their activities.

The newspaper *Irish Freedom* had been suppressed under the Defence of the Realm Act (DORA) in December 1914. Yet while the Fianna (amongst other organisations) were thereby robbed of a valuable platform, two enterprising Fianna members, Percy Reynolds and Patsy O'Connor, established *Fianna* in 1915. This was an unofficial paper and its circulation (over a thousand by February 1916) was less than a quarter that of *Irish Freedom* at its peak; but a quarter was better than nothing.[93] It was modeled on the British genre of boys' periodicals, but its concerns and preoccupations resonated with its intended audience in the ranks of the Fianna: a concentration on history, on the distinctiveness of Irish culture and a resistance to Anglicisation. The emphasis was on crucial attributes (such as patriotism) that were to be inculcated in the youth who were to be the future of the nationalist movement. It also provided another vehicle for reporting on the activities of the Fianna. Their *Ard-fheis* of 11 July 1915, held once again in the Mansion House, saw a further public sign of their militancy. A resolution was passed stating that a .22 rifle be adopted as the weapon of all third-class scouts. This was explicitly based on the practice of the American Boy Scouts; presumably, they were the same type of rifles as those held in the hall on Camden Street, though whether the resolution was prompted by the presence of the rifles, rather than the other way round, is unclear. The resolution also suggested that 'a musketry test be incorporated in the Fianna tests henceforth.' Heuston, as honorary treasurer, presented a report on the organisation's finances, 'which was considered satisfactory.'

The Fianna were now reorganised and a 'Headquarters' Staff' was appointed. After all, 'the movement was essentially a military one and from the resolutions the Congress had passed … it was their desire to have it even more military than ever.' This particular resolution passed despite the opposition of Bulmer Hobson, who 'contended that there was a civil side in the Fianna which was of even greater importance than the military one.' Interestingly, given the manner in which Hobson's star had fallen since supporting John Redmond's successful attempt to seize control of the Irish Volunteers, his stance was supported by Barney Mellows (Liam's brother) and Colbert, who felt that the fostering of 'good citizenship' was of greater import 'than drill or even musketry.' In any case, a compromise was reached, whereby a council was elected and they would choose the new headquarters staff. Of thirteen so elected, seven ended up on the headquarters staff. One of them was Heuston ('Mac Aodha'), who was now appointed Director of Training and was re-elected to the Central Council.[94] He was also appointed vice commandant of the reorganised Dublin battalion of the Fianna, as well as the commandant of its 6th company, based on North Frederick Street.[95] Heuston's rise through the ranks of the Fianna was complete and from this point onwards, his attention was increasingly devoted to his role in the Volunteers. Prior to the Rising Heuston was in charge of D Company of the 1st Battalion of the Volunteers in Dublin, with Liam Murnane and Dick Balfe as his deputies.[96] One of his colleagues in D Company left an evocative portrait of him.

Patrick Stephenson was born at 26 Lower Gloucester Street – two doors away from Heuston – and had also been educated by the Christian Brothers at North Richmond

Street. After leaving school in 1910 he joined the McHale Branch of the Gaelic League, meeting at 91 Upper Dorset Street. [97] The activities of the League kept him in touch with advanced nationalism and, having failed the exam to become a clerk in Dublin corporation, Stephenson decided to fill his free time by joining the Volunteers, though perhaps not for purely political reasons: as he put it himself , 'the continued sight of my friends and acquaintances marching and drilling proved irresistible.'[98] In early 1915 he joined D Company at No. 5 Blackhall Street ('the Colmcille Branch of the Gaelic League'). And, 'to my great surprise the Captain turned out to be Seán Heuston whom I had last seen in O'Connell Schools, North Richmond Street, some eleven years before.'

Stephenson was an enthusiastic volunteer and he soon approached the section leader, Dick Balfe, about subscribing monies towards a rifle. Balfe informed Heuston, commenting on this 'unusual keenness' and Heuston took an interest, especially as Stephenson had proven to be good at foot drill. According to Stephenson:

> When I told him I had learnt it at Richmond Street, he smiled and said, 'Now I remember, I was wondering where I had seen you before.' The abrupt, efficient officer became a cordial human being and after a few minutes chatting he went away with Dick. I left that night full, for the first time in my long life of twenty years, of a sense of belonging to something worthwhile and enjoying a sense of well being,

which later I was to understand derived from that quality of leadership and greatness that Seán and his like possess, and which they communicated to those they commanded. [99]

Stephenson was also acquainted, thanks to the Gaelic League, with another of those executed after the Rising: Edward Daly, 'a fine figure of a man with a rather serious looking face and sad eyes. In his well-tailored uniform he looked every inch a soldier. The combination of the soldierly figure with the pale complexion and the dark moustache created havoc among the ladies, while his smart military bearing inspired great respect in the minds of the rank and file of the battalion.'[100] But, he recalled, on the other hand,

Heuston was a violent contrast to our dapper commandant, a low-sized stocky figure attired in a brown tweed knicker-bocker suit with thick-soled boots. On the march and even when walking he had a habit of striking down hard with his left foot, as if marking time. The heavy dark eyebrows drawn down in a perpetual frown with the large full lips gave him a somewhat forbidding, almost ugly, appearance, which was quickly dissipated when the rare smile lit up his face, with a clear boyish gaiety. In this he was like Daly as also in that constant calm exterior which concealed depths of great strength and passion.[101]

Some of those who knew him recalled the five foot seven Heuston as a genial and pleasant individual;[102] others, that he was 'a very serious type, always wanting to do serious work; he had no time for singing or dancing.'[103] According to Prendergast,

> though he attained prominence in the different national spheres, it could not be said that he was a 'lime lighter' or pushed himself to the forefront; rather he was by nature unassuming and reserved. How often had we noticed, rather ruefully and not a little sadly, his coming on parade without his full Fianna uniform. To our amazement he would display his hat, which we often perceived he had tucked away under a loose rainproof coat that he usually wore or covered in brown paper. His light raincoat covered his uniform, tunic, haversack, water bottle etc. Seán always wore knee breeches and substantial woollen cycling stockings. His raincoat would then be tucked away in his haversack when on parade.
>
> After parade Seán returned to civilian attire, returning home as he came. He wore strong easy fitting boots of a military type, such as were made by Malone's of North King Street. This question of being well and suitably shod was one of Seán's big points; so strong was it with him, and of such importance, that he was never known to suffer from foot ailments or tiredness, which, as he often impressed on us, could be so easily attributable to indifferent footwear and want of proper hygiene. Many a lecture he gave us on these

same matters. He also was a fluent speaker of the native language. We were given a proof of this one night when a blind man, a friend of the Fianna and other national bodies, named Frank McGinty came to our hall and engaged Seán in conversation for a considerable time, much to our great surprise, for although we knew that he possessed a good knowledge of it we hardly thought that he was so fluent.[104]

Heuston's attitude to more serious matters could be almost playful. He was somewhat wary of being shadowed by 'G-men' (detectives from the DMP's G Division, with responsibility for political policing: hence the nickname), and enjoyed playing cat and mouse games to shake off their unwanted attention. On one occasion he drew a detective away from the Volunteer headquarters on Dawson Street by bringing a wrapped parcel resembling a rifle with him around the city; Heuston eventually revealed to the luckless detective that he had wasted his time by throwing the parcel into the Liffey near Queen Street bridge.[105]

Heuston and Balfe (whom Stephenson recalled as 'very earnest and efficient officers') had the job of training scouts and placed a great emphasis on fieldcraft, map-reading and observational skills as as they did so; Finglas and Santry were favoured locations for putting these skills to the test.[106] Scouting was not the only thing that they practised: according to Fionán Lynch, who commanded one of the neighbouring units of the volunteers, on one occasion in the spring of 1916 their battalion departed from the usual habit of drilling in north County Dublin and 'had a very important rehearsal in the heart of the city, actually over the ground which the battalion occupied in Easter Week. Seán Heuston was in charge of one half of the battalion and I was in charge of the other.'[107]

It was becoming increasingly obvious that the Volunteers in Dublin seemed to be going in a direction that strongly implied that action of some kind was imminent. Stephenson recalled that after a parade in Finglas which was flagged as the last of its kind until a 'serious situation should develop', suspicions that something was in the works became more widespread.[108] Indeed, in early 1916 a 'Fianna Commando' was apparently established, 'composed entirely of officers and older boys, formed in preparation for the coming conflict.' Heuston was initially supposed to be in charge of this, but his services were required by the Volunteers instead. The commando never materialised during the Rising itself, thanks to the countermanding order published on Easter Sunday 1916, but some members were involved in the abortive attack on the Magazine Fort in the Phoenix Park.[109]

Suspicions that something was imminent were fuelled by the fact that, in early 1916, the Volunteers were moving weapons around the city with increasing frequency. Heuston had appointed Stephenson as company quartermaster in late 1915. He later recalled that weapons were often moved around in an alarmingly indiscreet manner for, as Michael Staines, the quartermaster-general, put it, 'the more openly you do it the less you'll be suspected.' Weapons, or the lack thereof, were a continual headache for the Volunteers. But there were various ways of obtaining them and Stephenson witnessed a particularly brazen instance of Heuston doing so at remarkably close quarters:

On another occasion, having arrived rather early for parade I found Seán Heuston in the hall wearing a brown overcoat which reached almost to his feet. I do not know whether it was his own or if he had borrowed it for the occasion. However, he gave me a small revolver and some ammunition and told me to load it and put the rest of the bullets in my pocket. He then told me to come with him as far as the Broadstone. We set out together, walking along Queen Street, North King Street and up Constitution Hill. No word passed between us until we arrived in front of the Broadstone Terminus. We entered the station at the left and when we were at the gate he said 'Keep your eye on me and keep me covered in case anything happens.' A train had just pulled in and a party of British Tommies was getting out of the carriages. They threw their kit bags and equipment on a heap on the platform, left their rifles resting against the station wall, and went into what was probably a canteen or refreshment room, leaving their kit unprotected. From where I stood at the iron gate I watched Seán march down along the platform, as if he were on parade ground until he reached the spot where the rifles were leaning against the wall. With a quick look around, he opened his overcoat, whipped up a rifle, put it under the coat, turned quickly around and marched back and out of the station. As he came abreast of me he said, without pausing in his stride, 'come on', and out we went. To the present day I cannot remember what, if anything, happened after that except that when we got back to Colmcille he took the revolver and ammunition and went upstairs with the rifle.[110]

Heuston's company of the volunteers – 'D' – was small ('the penny company'), having been founded as an offshoot of the larger A Company.[111] According to Stephenson all of them, bar one, 'was living by what he earned by manual or clerical labour from week to week'; D Company were, quite literally, men of no property. But

> they were filled with the sense of an impending severe test
> for which a great reserve of strength would be required and
> for which they must be fit when it came. They were pos-
> sessed of a high degree of idealism – but they would have
> laughed at anyone who ventured to point this out.[112]

Stephenson remembered interminable discussions about getting weapons and gear, about 'new ideas on equipment or rations', though the 'more practical minded left the problem of equipment to those higher up and had a quiet evening's fun playing spoil five or solo, or in a solemn discussion of a hot tip for the 3 o'clock at Baldoyle being worth the modest investment of a shilling each way.'[113] He also recalled the perennially hassled battalion armourer, whose job was

> to make a Martini take Lee Enfield ammunition or make serviceable some antediluvian type of revolver that had been in somebody's family from ould God's time. The faith in this man's ability and ingenuity was astounding. Of his own limitations he was only too painfully aware and when his patience was exhausted he used to take refuge behind an explosive protest that 'he would be killed by all the work thrown on him before he had time to have a belt at the bloody British.'[114]

And, crucially, 'at this time it was generally accepted that this was what lay behind all the marching and drilling.'[115]

Chapter 5:

The Prelude to the Rising

Before his execution, Heuston assured his brother Michael that he had not been on any of the 'councils ... or committees or anything of that sort' prior to the Rising, and that he had only definitely found out that it was to take place on Easter Monday, though he 'had strong suspicions for about a week before, as we were moving a lot of stuff everywhere.'[116] Stephenson concurred: the intensified moving of material at Holy Week – the week just prior to Easter – 'created a feeling amounting to conviction that something serious was underfoot', though Heuston revealed nothing to those under him.[117]

But Heuston did reveal his suspicions to others. Some time before the Rising he had apparently intimated to Seán McLoughlin that something might happen on the Easter weekend and on Spy Wednesday – the Wednesday of Easter week – he told one woman in whose house the volunteers sometimes met – a 'Mrs Houlihan', who was presumably

Patrick Holohan's mother – that a rebellion was to take place at Easter.[118] Other hints of imminent action mounted during the week. Charles McQuaile, a member of the volunteers who also worked in the GPO, recalled that

> on Holy Thursday of Easter Week in the course of official duties I saw by accident on the desk of the Superintendent's clerk an official paper headed 'Secret and Confidential' with the address 'Dublin Castle'.

The gist of this document was to the effect that a 'round up' of Volunteer Leaders and prominent Sinn Féiners was to take place at Easter Sunday midnight.'[119] Whether this was related to the so-called 'Castle Document', which purported to reveal plans for an impending round-up of radical nationalists, is unclear; the Castle Document was based on existing British contingency plans that were to be implemented if conscription was imposed in Ireland.[120] What McQuaile saw was a despatch to Arthur Hamilton Norway, the secretary of the Irish Post Office, instructing that suburban post offices 'would have some member of staff in attendance to admit members of the police and military only on Easter Sunday night and Easter Monday.' By April 1916 the British authorities had become increasingly suspicious of the motives of the Volunteers, though as they did not feel that any rebellion was imminent, they declined to clamp down on them. But after the abortive attempt to import weapons on the *Aud*, the

British stance changed: when Dublin Castle was attacked on Easter Monday, the Under-Secretary, Sir Matthew Nathan, was discussing the possibility of finally suppressing the Volunteers, and one of those at the relevant meeting was Arthur Hamilton Norway.[121] In those circumstances, what McQuaile saw was unlikely to have been a forgery.

McQuaile had to parade at Blackhall Street that evening and

> recognising the significance of the document I had seen in the GPO. I mentioned the matter to my Company Officer, [Liam] Murnane. He instructed me to see Seán Heuston … This I did and Heuston asked me if these papers could be got. I said it might be possible adding that the most likely place where they would be held would be in the Secretary's Office and if we could get down there before 9pm, before the cleaners left off, we would be able to get into the office direct.

McQuaile and Heuston went to the GPO with this objective in mind and, 'arriving there we found, amongst a lot of other papers, the document [for] which we were searching. We took this document which referred to the arrests and we went across to an address in Dawson Street'; the Volunteer Headquarters at Number Two.

> We went up a stairway. Heuston said, 'You hang back a minute' and he went into the room. In a short time Mr

Tom Clarke and Bulmer Hobson emerged, also [Seán] Mac-
Dermott and [Eoin] MacNeill. [John] McBride was there too
… This would be somewhere between 9 and 9.30pm. Heuston
came out and more or less dismissed me with the remark 'It was
a good night's work.'[122]

The next day, Good Friday, Heuston was involved in
moving what he described as 'whole cart load' of ammunition from a house in Prussia Street, which seemed to
have convinced him that the Rising was now imminent; he
had instructed a member of the Fianna, [Joe?] Cullen, to
deliver errands across the city, which included the delivery
of large and unwieldy ammunition boxes to Liberty Hall.[123]
On Holy Saturday arms and ammunition continued to be
moved from hiding places to be stored in the hall in Blackhall Place, under an armed guard led by Heuston.[124] Stephenson kept the company's 'meagre reserve of ammunition
and equipment' in a shop called Kane's in Stoneybatter (he
later married the owner's daughter).[125] At the Colmcille Hall
Stephenson encountered Heuston. Stephenson recalled that

[Heuston] told me he had heard there was a rifle, ammunition and a complete British soldiers kit to be got at Usher's
Quay and asked me to come with him to help him carry it
back. In a lane behind Ganly's we found a young lad about
eighteen dressed in khaki and sitting huddled up beside a
roaring fire in the front room of a small house. He looked

the picture of misery and his uniform was still mud-stained.
He told us he was going to desert and wanted to get rid of
his equipment. Seán handed two pounds to the woman of
the house – obviously his mother. We got a Lee Enfield and
short bayonet, a set of web equipment with the pouches full
of 303 clips and a sniper's canvas sling similarly stuffed with
303. We shook hands with the woman and the boy, and
wishing him luck returned to Blackhall Street.[126]

Heuston then gave Stephenson two pounds and told him
'that is all that's left of the company funds you had better
take charge of it, we may want to buy food on Sunday.'[127]
Presumably, the suspicions that Heuston later intimated to
his brother had intensified; this may also have coloured what
happened the next day.

On Easter Sunday, Heuston was told about Eoin Mac-
Neill's cancellation of the scheduled Volunteer manoeuvres by James Brennan, who had bought the *Sunday Independent* before calling into Heuston on Fontenoy Street.
His response to Brennan was, 'This is terrible. Go get your
breakfast and come down to 41 Parnell Square.' Brennan did
so and found Volunteers milling around in confusion, before
they were eventually told to go home and wait for developments.[128] Later, on the instructions of Connolly, Pearse and
MacDonagh, Michael Staines went to the headquarters of
the Volunteer's 3rd Battalion – led by Éamon de Valera – to
tell them that MacDonagh was calling off their mobilisa-

tion in the wake of MacNeill's countermanding order. Heuston went with him. On hearing this, de Valera was sceptical and threatened to imprison Staines and gave no indication that he would obey this new instruction. Heuston 'was very indignant and told me afterwards that he was almost on the point of drawing his gun.'[129] According to Staines:

> Heuston and I felt that the cancellation had ruined everything and he suggested that we should go to some peaceful place and talk it over ... We were downhearted. We were both keen on going on with it, but there was nothing to do but await orders.[130]

They went up to Pine Forest to discuss what had happened. The encounter with de Valera had shaken both of them quite badly.

> It particularly affected Heuston who kept on repeating, 'Michael, it's horrible, it's horrible'...We discussed the thing fully and looked at it more calmly and coolly than if we had been in town, listening to people talking.[131]

This was a fair point. Stephenson had also been taken aback by what MacNeill had done and went to the Colmcille Hall, where there 'was an atmosphere of great excitement and futile speculation, a great deal of criticism of the chief of staff and no orders.' In the absence of any definite instructions, Stephenson went to Kane's for his dinner and then for a walk in the Phoenix Park.[132] Ignatius Callender was also surprised by what he had read in that morning's papers; it struck him as highly unusual, given the efficiency with which the Volunteers were usually mobilised. He too went to the Colmcille Hall to find various confused Volunteers milling around seeking confirmation of what had gone on, along with 'dozens of boxes of ammunitions and high explosives.'[133] Heuston and Staines returned to Blackhall Street at around 3pm that afternoon and had also 'found Heuston's company mobilised there. They remained mobilised in Blackhall Street all that Sunday night and Heuston remained with them. There were members of other companies there also.'[134] Heuston (who, according to Staines, had been 'jumping with tension' that day) told Callender to inform any members of his company who might turn up to remain in the hall for further instructions. At around 8pm, he attended a meeting behind closed doors in the hall with Edward Daly and number of others; after an hour they all left, except Heuston. [135]

Stephenson attended the 'usual Sunday night *ceilidhe*' in the hall, but recalled that it seemed to have an unusally charged atmosphere. Later, at around midnight ('towards the end of the night's fun'), Heuston and a number of others went out to check that no detectives – 'G men' – were watching the hall. He then sent most of them home, but remained there himself, having asked a number of Volunteers – Stephenson, Balfe, Liam Staines, Frank Cullen, Eddie Roach and Joe Byrne – to help guard the hall lest it be raided that night: they were to return after everyone had gone home, checking that no detectives were in the area. Stephenson recalled that the usual detective (a man called Culhane, from the west of Ireland, who lived nearby, was on good terms with them and was suspected by Stephenson to sympathise with their cause) was nowhere to be seen as they returned. And 'just before lights out, Seán Heuston came in and joined us. He examined a huge German Mauser pistol and having satisfied himself that it was in working order switched off the lights and lay down with us.'[136]

That evening, before midnight, a letter arrived at 20 Fontenoy Street for Heuston. According to Michael Heuston their mother took it, but at around 12.20am a note from Seán arrived, 'saying he was at the Hall, would not be home and not to wait up for him. Mother told the Volunteer that another letter had come for him and to bring it back with him. He said the Hall was surrounded by detectives and he might not be able to get back and that it would be better for her to open it and remember the message in case he could not deliver it.' She found a note from Pearse and MacDonagh, instructing Heuston to be at Liberty Hall at 8am with, as they termed it, 'four orderlies and four cyclists'. [137]

The message was relayed to Blackhall Street early the next morning. The Volunteers in the hall were awakened by loud knocking and, suspecting a raid, Heuston cocked his gun and told the others to stay put. He went downstairs and no sounds came up. After some time he returned, flushed, and with the message that had been delivered. 'You may all go back to sleep,' he said, 'I'll want a couple of you to go to Liberty Hall at eight o'clock this morning to act as despatch carriers.'[138] Stephenson went back to sleep, was awakened by Staines, was made ill by a hardboiled egg at breakfast and was then sent by Heuston to Liberty Hall, from where he and the others were to deliver messages across the city.

What Stephenson and the others were doing was delivering orders to bring out as many of the Volunteers as could be mustered at short notice on Easter Monday. Heuston did the same. At around 10am he returned to the family home on Fontenoy Street, 'in a hurry and ran in saying excitedly, "We're going to have the parade after all".' Michael Heuston recalled

He [Seán] removed the boards and began to take out the ammunition from the place in which he kept it and to put it in a pile on the floor. 'What are you taking out that for?' said mother. 'Wasn't it alright where it was?' 'We'll want it all for the parade.' 'I thought you weren't going to take that till "The Day"? said Duckie; to which she received no answer.

He ate hardly any breakfast. 'Why didn't you eat your breakfast?' said mother. 'Did you get anything in the Hall?'

'Oh, yes, we got eggs and things this morning.'

He then took out the new hat he had bought for the parade, and went out. When he was gone, mother put back the ammunition, replacing the boards.[139]

It seems that Teresa Heuston had a very clear understanding of what her eldest brother had been preparing to do for some time.

On the morning of Easter Monday, D Company paraded at the junction of Temple Street and Hardwicke Street; Stephenson attended with the equipment he and Heuston had bought from the deserting Tommy. He noted the bank holiday atmosphere, with cars racing up Stoneybatter en route to Fairyhouse at a strikingly early hour. He then went to the assembly point to find that little more than a third of the company had turned up. On returning to Blackhall Place the previous day, Heuston had ordered Stephenson to mobilise two members who had been 'excused parades'; there were to be as few exceptions to his mobilisation as possible.[140] It was obvious, on the Monday morning, that this attention to detail had not had the desired effect, but

soon after Heuston came round from Dorset Street wearing a Sam Browne belt over the same old brown tweed suit of knickerbockers wearing a green Fianna hat that was a size too small for his head. It made him look slightly ridiculous and we could not but smile at him. He was completely undisturbed by this and without any delay gave us the orders to fall in.[141]

Those who did turn up were James Brennan, Seán Derrington, Liam Derrington, Joe Byrne, Eddie Roach, Frank Cullen, Willie O'Dea, Thomas O'Kelly, Dick Balfe, Liam Staines, Liam Murnane, Stephenson and Heuston himself: thirteen from D Company, with Seán McLoughlin of the Fianna in tow.[142] There was also Charles McQuaile, who had been instructed to deliver some ammunition to Heuston at St Georges Church, just off Dorset Street, from his home in Stoneybatter; having done so, Heuston then told him to remain there as the company moved off and to tell any late-comers that they were to go to Liberty Hall.[143]

They marched to Liberty Hall and assembled in front of it. Heuston went inside and Stephenson took the chance to look over the other groups assembled outside: members of the Citizen Army in olive green uniforms with green leather kit, although their soldierly bearing was offset by the sloppiness of their 'blue check cotton haversacks'. He also noted some in civilian clothes, 'a large number of the famous Howth Mausers', along with double-barreled shotguns; those in civilian clothes had more of the latter and he also thought that he saw a numbers of 'pikes or lances'.[144] Heuston came back out, looking 'very pleased', called his men to attention, 'formed us into fours and putting himself at the head gave us the order 'quick march'.[145]

They crossed Butt Bridge and turned right. The column encountered Ignatius Callendar at Burgh Quay, who fell in at Heuston's command; their conversation went unheard, but he dropped out.[146] Callendar had been planning on going to the Colmcille Hall that morning, but his breakfast was interrupted by a request from Seán MacDiarmada to deliver a message to John MacBride (his superior in the corporation); he was on his way to do so when he encountered Heuston and D Company on Burgh Quay. Having been told to 'fall in', Callender explained his errand and Heuston told him that on the way back he should collect some pistols in Eden Quay, find Michael Staines and report back to Heuston at his eventual destination.[147] The rest of the column were, however, none the wiser as to where this actually was. They marched on in speculative silence, listening for instructions to turn left or right; none came. They were joined by two more members, Fred Brooks and George Levins. As they neared Skipper's Alley 'curiosity got the better of us' and they began to speak amongst themselves, with some skepticism: 'this is all a bloody cod', said one 'we're going back to Colmcille, the damn thing is off again.'[148] By now they had reached Church Street Bridge. Stephenson was convinced that they were returning to the hall, but when they did not cross the river his confusion returned. It did not last: when they drew abreast of the Mendicity Institution on Usher's Island 'Seán turned right about, faced us and shouted "Company left wheel, seize this building and hold it in the name of the Irish Republic."'[149]

• • • • •

Chapter 6:

The Mendicity Institution

The building that Heuston had been ordered to capture was the Mendicity Institution, located on the south quays of the Liffey at Usher's Island, west of the city centre. It was originally built in 1752 as the Dublin residence of John Rawdon, first earl of Moira. The second earl, Francis Rawdon-Hastings, had been a senior officer in the British army and saw service in the American Revolution, where his aide-de-camp was his fellow Irishman (and future United Irishman) Lord Edward Fitzgerald; Fitzgerald apparently visited Moira House on a number of occasions prior to his arrest in 1798. There was another republican association around the corner from the building, at the top of Bridgefoot Street, where Robert Emmet was executed outside St Catherine's Church in 1803.

The area around the Mendicity Institution also had a significant literary association. The eighteenth-century townhouse at no. 15 Usher's Island, located a few metres west of the Mendicity, was the home of two maiden aunts of James Joyce in the 1890s and was immortalised as the setting of his short story 'The Dead'. The final story in Joyce's classic collection, *Dubliners* (originally published in 1914), 'The Dead' revolves around a dinner party on the feast of the Epiphany (6 January) attended by Gabriel Conroy and his wife, Gretta, and hosted by his maiden aunts Kate and Julia Morkan in their 'dark gaunt house on Usher's Island'.[150] Like so much of Joyce's writing, 'The Dead' is filled with subtle metaphor and symbolism and the west of Ireland is a recurring motif in the story: Gabriel Conroy is chided by an old friend, Molly Ivors, as a 'West Briton', due to his lack of interest in both the west and the Irish language; his wife, Gretta, is from Galway; and ultimately, Gabriel Conroy comes to be haunted by a ghost from the west of Ireland, in the shape of a story from his wife's past. But despite this concentration on the far west, just a few metres east of the house in which the story is set is a building that opens a window on a world conspicuously absent from that of 'The Dead': that of Dublin's inner city poor, as ministered to by the Mendicity Institution.

In 1818 a number of concerned citizens established an 'Association for the prevention and suppression of Mendicity in Dublin'.[151] Traditionally, charity in Dublin was left to the Churches and to wealthy benefactors; the new organisation would depend upon the latter. Dublin was no stranger to poverty, but this problem had increased in the years after the

Above: Heuston's parents, John and Maria (née McDonald).

Left: John Heuston, Sean's father.

Right: Heuston as a member of Na Fianna Éireann. The photo was taken at the Fianna *Ard-Fheis* of 1913.

Right: Heuston in civilian attire.

Below: The Fianna *Ard-Fheis* held in Dublin's Mansion House on 13 July 1913. Heuston is seated in the second row, third from the left.

Above: Constance Markievicz, in suitably Gaelic attire. Along with Bulmer Hobson, she helped to found the Fianna in Dublin in 1909.

Left: Application form for the Irish Volunteers, founded in Dublin in November 1913.

Below: Members of the Fianna waiting to receive weapons being unloaded from the Asgard at Howth Pier, 26 July 1914.

Moira House Dublin

Opposite top: An engraving of Moira House, originally published in 1811. The house later became the Mendicity Institution.

Opposite bottom: Kingsbridge: the massive Dublin terminus of the Great Southern and Western Railway was built in the 1840s. Heuston worked there from September 1913 onwards; it was later renamed after him.

Above: A group of Republicans at the Fianna Hall in Limerick, circa 1913. John Daly is seated in the middle of the first row. Heuston and Con Colbert are standing at the back, third and fourth from the right respectively.

Above: British troops waiting at Kingstown (Dun Laoghaire) train station. Note the amount of mail bags awaiting delivery as there had been no post during the Rising.

Act of Union of 1801. The city had been rebuilt in the eight-eenth century by the Anglican aristocracy usually described as the 'ascendancy'. These Protestant landowners had been the beneficiaries of the seventeenth-century conquest of Ire-land, but many – like the earls of Moira – retained houses in Dublin. Dublin was the capital, after all, and was the location of the parliament in which so many of the 'ascendancy' sat. Even for those who did not sit in parliament, Dublin exerted a magnetic pull as a centre of society and style; a place to see and to be seen in. But the Act of Union had helped to bring this world to an end: with the abolition of the parlia-ment, the aristocracy gradually abandoned the city, usually in favour of London and this had two significant consequences. The first was that the elegant townhouses built as their urban residences (which they had also abandoned) fell into decay; a century later, many would be squalid tenements. The second was that the services industries and consumer culture that developed around the parliament and gentry also faded away. Within the new United Kingdom local industries such as textile manufacturing, a traditional staple of the Liberties, could not compete with Britain's industrial revolution.[152] As Dublin declined in the years after the union, the problem of poverty got worse.

The new charity was aimed at stamping out 'mendicity' – begging. It was to operate across the city and its emphasis was on promoting self-sufficiency, rather than just providing charity: training in trades, for example, was to be provided. In its early years the association had been moved around a number of premises in Dawson Street, Hawkins Street and Copper Alley. But the former townhouse of the earls of Moira was deemed to be most suitable of a number of buildings that were inspected with an eye to providing a more permanent home (the second earl relocated to London after 1801 and in 1812 had been appointed governor-general of Bengal, in India). The house was not perfect: there were concerns that it might be too far from the city centre and some local residents complained that its new role might lower the tone of the area. When a nine-hundred-year lease was signed in December 1823, it stipulated that a wall was to be built between the house and the quays, and that those using it were to enter by the back entrance on Island Street (a condition that still applies today). The Mendicity Institution would provide schooling, food and training for the urban poor (as well as, from 1848, Dublin's first public bath). The downward spiral that the city embarked upon in the nineteenth-century meant that there was no shortage of patrons.

And it is this that probably explains its absence from Joyce's story. His famous attention to detail meant that he was unlikely to have been unaware of what was located beside his aunts house. 'The Dead' is filled with allusions to both Irish history and Irish nationalism,[153] but the story itself is infused with another issue: class. The two aunts, Kate and

Julia, had moved to the 'dark gaunt house' from Stoneybatter, which was, in social terms, a step down in the world. Despite their age, they were still working as, respectively, a music teacher and a soprano. Their niece Mary Jane, who lived with them ('the main prop of the household'), was also a music teacher and many of her pupils 'belonged to the better-class families on the Kingstown and Dalkey line'; she might have been trying to move back up in the world.[154] This trait may have run in the family: as Gabriel Conroy leaves he tells a story about a disastrous attempt by his grandfather Patrick Morkan to 'drive out with the quality' – the upper classes – and Aunt Kate interjects to reassure those listening that he 'had a starch mill' and wasn't the 'glue-boiler' her nephew claims him to be. When Gabriel mentions that his grandfather had 'his ancestral mansion somewhere near Back Lane', at the edge of the Liberties, Aunt Kate jumps in to correct him once again: Grandfather Patrick did not live in Back Lane, as 'only the mill was there'.[155] Gabriel's grandfather might have been long gone, but his Aunt Kate was still keeping up his appearances.

Despite his aunts' straitened circumstances, the Christmas dinner that Gabriel and the other guests had just tucked into was extraordinarily opulent: 'a fat brown goose', 'a round of spiced beef, 'two little minsters of jelly, red and yellow', 'blancmange and red jam', 'peeled almonds' and 'a solid rectangle of Smyrna figs', 'chocolates and sweets wrapped in gold and silver papers', 'a pyramid of oranges and American apples' and, last but not least, 'three squads of bottles of stout and ale and minerals'.[156] It was in stark contrast to the more humble fare on offer a few doors up from the house; in the early years of the twentieth century the reality was that the Mendicity served its patrons 'stirabout and milk for breakfast and bread and soup made from ox heads for dinner'; even then, there were still complaints that the staff kept the meat from the ox heads for themselves.[157]

The poverty that the Mendicity Institution represented was not part of the world of Dublin's middle classes; the kind of people who attended the Morkan sisters' dinner party in 'The Dead'. The poor were not noticed by the inhabitants of this fictional world, nor were they included by its creator. But Gabriel Conroy did notice, in his after-dinner speech, the presence of 'a new generation growing up in our midst, a generation actuated by new ideas and new principles. It is serious and enthusiastic for these new ideas and its enthusiasm, even when it is misdirected, is, I believe, in the main sincere.'[158]

He may well have been speaking of the generation that Heuston and his colleagues were a part of. Whatever about their enthusiasm being misdirected, given that they went to Usher's Island on 24 April 1916 fully intending to fight for their 'new ideas and new principles', they were undoubtedly serious – or 'sincere' – about what they were doing.

Joyce wrote *Dubliners* at roughly the same time as the Boer War, during which the number of men using the Mendicity declined (though it increased again once the war was over). Around this time, in 1898, James Connolly himself wrote an account of the 'hopeless misery and unfeeling charity' that characterised the building, written with a level of detail that suggested some familiarity with it.[159] The introduction of the old age pension in 1908 had eased the burden on the institution, though the 1913 Lockout saw the numbers using it increase. Its use declined again during the First World War, given that the levels of recruitment from Dublin meant that wages were now flowing into the city. But the Mendicity still had a job to do: in 1916 alone, 22,709 men, women and children availed of its services.[160] It was perhaps ironic that the republicans who were making for it on 24 April were being led by a young man who had grown up in the poverty of the tenements. Had Heuston not held down a job with the GSWR, he and his family might have availed of its services themselves.

James Connolly had ordered Heuston to take the building. But why? Indeed, why had Heuston been chosen to take it? The second of these questions is the more difficult to answer. Michael Cremen claimed that he and Heuston were originally instructed to seize Aldborough House (which was occupied by the Post Office) on Easter Sunday.[161] Alternatively, 'he was sent to the Mendicity Institute to replace an officer who failed to turn out.'[162] Dick Balfe later told Michael Heuston that Seán had been promoted prior to the Rising, but that this was never publicised amidst the preparations.[163] Michael Staines later confirmed this to Michael Heuston; that a makeshift 'headquarters battalion' was to be created for the Rising out of some of the existing Volunteer companies, but 'probably the arrangement was never put in writing, as little was ever written. Jack was to be commandant.'[164] In any case, Heuston ended up bypassing any regular command structure and instead reported directly to Connolly and Pearse in the GPO. The irregularity of these arrangements is hinted at in Liam Tannam's novel take on why Heuston ended up in charge of the Mendicity Institution:

> About five or six weeks before the Rising Thomas Mac-Donagh asked me and Seán Heuston to attend at 2 Dawson Street for special lectures on house fighting, but I was too busy with my company and my girl and so failed to attend these lectures. Seán Heuston did attend and I believe that's why he got charge of the Mendicity Institute in Easter Week.[165]

But the reason for choosing Heuston to take the building seems lost amidst the confusion that accompanied the outbreak of the Rising and the machinations of the organisations involved in it.

There is less confusion about the choice of building. The attraction of the Mendicity Institution to the Volunteers was its location. The building was on the Liffey, on the fringes of one of Dublin's only industrial areas. This was ironic, as the relative absence of major industries from Dublin was a cause of so much of its notorious poverty in the first place. The area directly behind the Mendicity was dominated by brewing and distilling; most famously the massive Guinness complex (totally rebuilt in the 1870s), but also a number of smaller and now long-departed establishments: the Anchor Brewery on Usher Street, the Powers and Roe distilleries on Thomas Street and, last but not least, the Ardee Street brewery of Watkins, Jameson, Pim & Co. Ltd, which was occupied during the Rising by Volunteers under Con Colbert. The production of vast quantities of alcohol employed thousands and gave this part of the city a unique character.[166] On the other hand, the existence of this huge industrial area meant that it was not the most fashionable of localities; another sign, perhaps, that the Morkan sisters in 'The Dead' were slowly but surely moving down in the world. But the brewing and distilling quarter lay behind Usher's Island. Heuston's occupation of the Mendicity had far more to do with what was happening at the front, on the other side of the Liffey.

The GPO occupies a central role in the imagery of the Rising, but from the point of view of the British forces who suppressed it, the most serious fighting they faced in Dublin was at Mount Street Bridge and around the Four Courts, another of the great public buildings of the eighteenth-century city.[167] The area was occupied by Volunteers led by Edward Daly, who would be the youngest of those executed after the Rising; Heuston was born a week after him. Unlike Heuston, however, Daly came from a notably republican family: John Daly was his uncle and his sister, Kathleen, married Tom Clarke, who would be the first signatory of the Proclamation. These connections were unlikely to have hindered his rapid ascent through the ranks of the Volunteers, but Daly turned out to be both capable and, crucially, thorough. The latter trait proved essential, given the scale of what he and the Volunteers in his charge had been tasked with doing. Daly and his men were to hold both the Four Courts and an area running north along Church Street, past Broadstone Station towards Cabra, west towards Smithfield and Brunswick Street, and finally east towards Bolton Street; parts of the city that Heuston would have been very famil-iar with. Like the Volunteers elsewhere, Daly's 1st Battalion, which had assembled in Blackhall Place on the morning of 24 April, was hampered by the relatively small numbers that had turned out (less than a third of the whole, in this case); over the next few days they would be forced to compensate for this in inventive ways.

The reason for taking the area around the Fourt Courts was to interfere with the movement of troops into the city, which was bound to be a certainty as the Rebellion progressed. The actual military strategy of the Rising is, like so much else that was discussed amongst the leadership, virtually impossible to discern, but here was one aspect of its planning that displayed common sense and foresight: the fact that the Volunteers made sure that they had occupied and covered the obvious points through which British reinforcements could enter the city. Hence the reason why the British authorities singled out Upper Mount Street and around the Four Courts as the areas where they experienced the heaviest fighting. Éamon de Valera's men in Boland's Bakery had established outposts overlooking Mount Street Bridge: an obvious bottleneck on an obvious route into the city that troops disembarking from Kingstown were likely to take; the inexperienced troops of the Sherwood Foresters did so and suffered appalling casualties as a result. Daly and his men, on the other side of the city, were in a similar situation, as there were major barracks and transport hubs located in the south and west of Dublin. Units of the Royal Dublin Fusiliers were in the Royal Barracks (now Collins Barracks), located on the Liffey near the Phoenix Park, while across the river was Kingsbridge Station: the obvious terminus should troops be brought up to Dublin from the Curragh. Ironically, Heuston's employer was instrumental in facilitating British reinforcements travelling to Dublin; the GSWR network had moved three thousand troops into Dublin by Tuesday night.[168]

The north western edge of the city posed similar challenges. Marlborough Barracks, just off the North Circular Road, housed large numbers of cavalry, while Broadstone Station was the Dublin terminus for the Midland Great Western Railway, who operated the main Dublin-Galway line: another possible route for reinforcements to reach Dublin. Broadstone was also located on high ground, which made it a potentially useful location for British counter-attacks. What Daly and his garrison had to do was hold a large and significant area of the city, one that contained a number of obvious pathways for British reinforcements heading towards O'Connell Street and he was to interfere with this as best he could. Daly's men were to be the first rebel line of defence in the north-west of the city. And this brings us back to the Mendicity Institution. Connolly had told Heuston to hold the building for a matter of hours, for a simple reason. If troops began to move towards the city centre from the Royal Barracks along the north quays, then the Mendicity Institution was an obvious vantage point from which the Volunteers could attack them, pin them down and enable Daly to get on with his own preparations around the Four Courts. Once these were complete, the Mendicity would be redundant and was to be abandoned. Heuston's brief was to buy time for Daly and his men. Yet as the men in his charge marched along the south quays from Liberty Hall, they were unaware of this purpose, of their destination and, above all, of the fact that they were going to be besieged inside it for the next three days.

Chapter 7:

• • • • •

Heuston's Fort

The Volunteers stormed the Mendicity Institution yelling and whooping; a relief from the 'pent-up feelings of bewilderment and frustration' that had built up along the march. Stephenson ended up in the caretaker's living quarters on the top floor with a number of others, including Dick Balfe and Liam Staines. The windows were smashed, as were china ornaments, vases, and a glass case full of stuffed birds: all were broken to prevent their shattering into shrapnel. Furniture was pushed up against the window frames. The curtains were torn down and wedged into the gap between the furniture and the sashes. 'Everything in the nature of cloth in the room was stuffed into the barricade at the window and anything likely to burn was jammed into the fireplace.'[169] A bucket of water was also brought into the room. Stephenson heard a woman scream in the house, along with 'hoarse cries and angry shouts as the unfortunate down and outs, denied their chance of their midday meal, were being hustled out of the basement dining hall, across the courtyard at the back and into Island Street at the point of the revolver.'[170] The minutes of the Institution recorded that:

> On Easter Monday April 24th, the Sinn Féiners, twenty-five in [the] charge of one of their officers, entered the institution by the side entrance, the principal entrance being closed on account of its being a holiday. The poor people had been admitted and were at their dinner in the dining hall. They immediately proceeded to drive them out. They next turned their attention to the occupants and servants of the institution: the superintendent with his family live on the premises and they were driven out at the point of a bayonet, not being allowed to carry anything with them.[171]

The Mendicity would serve no meals to anyone for the next three weeks. Some of those involved in its occupation later claimed that the building had been empty; perhaps due to a sense of embarrassment at having driven out the poor who relied on it for sustenance.[172] The back gate was shut against them. Heuston then detailed James Brennan and Joe Byrne to go to a house on Watling Street, to take up a position on an iron balcony. But this turned out to be unstable, so they returned to the Mendicity and remained there.[173]

Stephenson held a window at the end of a room facing the river. He stripped off his gear, sat in an armchair at the window and noticed a police officer with 'a big soft face with big eyes like those of an oxen' and 'a broad country accent' leaning against the front wall. The policeman called up to the volunteers.

'Eh, you fellows are going too far with this playing at soldiers. Don't you know you can be arrested for what yez are doing?'

Given the circumstances, Stephenson found this hilarious and burst out laughing. A voice from elsewhere in the building replied:

'Be off to hell out of that, if you don't want a bullet in your thick skull.'

The policeman did not move. The voice continued:

'You big eejit, why don't you take yourself off while you're alive. Don't you know the Republic has been proclaimed and your bloody day is done.' This was followed by a shot that sent the policeman running down the quays, losing his helmet as he did so. Stephenson

was still laughing when Heuston came into the room. He inspected the barricading of the windows and then told us that the Irish Republic was to be proclaimed at twelve noon at the GPO and that our job was to hold the Mendicity and engage any troops that would come out of the Royal Barracks across the river in Benburb Street until such time as the First Battalion, under Commandant Ned Daly, had taken over the Four Courts and had established itself there.[174]

110

Once that happened, Heuston and his men were to abandon the Mendicity, retreat to the waiting room of the Guinness Brewery at the corner of Watling Street, and make contact with Éamonn Ceannt in the South Dublin Union. Heuston ordered his men back to their posts and told them to wait.

> When the troops move out of the barracks wait until they are right opposite to you before opening fire. A single blast of my whistle will be the signal to fire.[175]

Heuston then took some of his men outside to construct a barricade, 'towards the city side of the building.[176]

Stephenson turned the back of the armchair to the window and knelt on the seat, resting the rifle on its back. From this vantage point he noticed that the trams were still running on the north quays. The quay in front of the Mendicity was deserted, but he saw that groups of people had clustered at the corners of Ellis Street, Blackhall Street, John Street, and Queen Street. All were observing the Mendicity.[177]

As he waited, Stephenson became somewhat pensive. He recalled Edward Fitzgerald's connection with the house, and remembered that he had booked seats for 'the Gondoliers for that night at the Gaiety.' But

> the contrast between the scented air, the bright lights and the lively music of the theatre and the atmosphere of shabbiness, decay and poverty in the Mendicity, coupled with

the grimness of the business that had us here, created a
heavy sense of depression that lay on me like a ton of lead.

He thought about previous failed insurrections, from
Owen Roe O'Neill to the Fenians, and how they had been
undermined by either informers, or a combination of weak
or divided leadership, or even both. At least in this case
the problem was not informers, which gave the Volunteers
the advantage of surprise. He also reflected upon the cold
reality of the situation: 'so far there was plenty of physical
discomfort, fatigue, sweat, and excitement, but damn little
romance.'[178]

Outside, Heuston was still attempting to construct a barricade; Seán McLoughlin recalled that they had stopped the
trams on the south quays at gunpoint and while material
was scarce they obtained carts 'from a neighbouring yard',
though one of the owners then tried to take his back at
the first opportunity. McLoughlin had to recruit unwilling members of the public at gunpoint to help out, but was
willing to argue with the disgruntled owner of the cart.[179]
Eventually the barricades were established, but they had just
been completed when the Volunteers were summoned back
inside as troops were spotted coming down the quays and
Stephenson was broken out of his revery by the sight of soldiers coming out of the Royal Barracks.[180]

According to Michael Heuston,

the troops emerging from the Royal Barracks were the 10th (Commercial) Battalion of the Royal Dublin Fusiliers, under the command of Lieutenant D.O.M. Keahy. They were inexperienced troops. The Volunteers, in the course of the fighting that soon broke out, saw officers instructing the soldiers how to use their rifles, which had not been loaded when they left the barracks. Despite this, they were being sent into the city in order to 'frighten the Sinn Féiners'.[181]

Despite the fact that Heuston and his men were holding the Mendicity Institution in order to attack any troops on their way past the Four Courts, the first soldiers they exchanged gunfire with were apparently en route to Dublin Castle, and their destination may have influenced their conduct.

They marched down the quays four deep, 'expecting nothing', but when they reached a spot on the quays between Ellis Street and Blackhall Place somebody on the ground floor of the Mendicity fired at them; Stephenson attributed this to nerves.[182] According to Balfe, the Volunteers had apparently been hanging out a tricolour flag that caught the attention of the officer at the head of the column, and he had pointed a sword at it but was shot dead; if this is what happened, then it may have caused some uncertainty on the part of the troops as to precisely where the firing was coming from.[183] The officer who had been shot – one of the first 'British' soldiers to be killed in the Rising – was in fact Irish. Gerald Neilan, a veteran of the Boer War, had been born in Rathmines; ironically, his younger brother Arthur was part of the Volunteer garrison in the Four Courts.[184]

When the troops were fired on they scattered and sought shelter wherever they could find, as they sought to regroup and return fire.[185] Most of the Volunteers' gunfire was coming from the upper story of the Mendicity, as it offered the most unobstructed views.[186] Heuston's whistle was soon lost in the din.[187] The trams on the north quays had stopped by now; the passengers had fled from one of them, so some of the troops took cover behind the empty vehicle. Stephenson recalled that after the first frenzied bursts of fire he took to sniping, with no response. This went on until a whistle was blown on the other side of the river and the troops retreated into the side streets. 'In the end the soldiers managed to escape, and they then bombed the mill and a publichouse (probably beside the mill) as they thought the Volunteers were there. Finding none, they thought they had escaped.'[188] The fighting was over in a matter of minutes.[189]

Heuston and his men took stock of their position. The Mendicity had been hit, but there were no casualties. It was quiet outside; traffic had stopped and the soldiers were nowhere to be seen, but knots of onlookers had gathered at the corners across the river.[190] Heuston ordered that a room at the back of the Mendicity be used for cooking and that its windows be blacked out with blankets and tablecloths. Stephenson found some food: tea, sugar, milk, rice, a plum pudding and a bottle of Guinness.[191] They continued to wait.

The accounts that some of the participants in the fighting at the Mendicity later provided to the Bureau of Military History differed on some details. This was to be expected, given that the testimonies were being recorded three decades after the event. According to Balfe, the Volunteers had let a small party of sappers pass down the north quays unmolested before the main column of troops emerged.[192] McLoughlin, on seeing that they were carrying picks and shovels rather than rifles, claimed to have told Heuston 'You are not going to shoot them', to which the reply was 'No, but we will fire over their heads and scatter them and give them a scare.'[193] But Stephenson claimed that they fired on the sappers after McLoughlin had left on an errand.[194]

The errand in question was done at Heuston's request: he had sent McLoughlin out to collect some homemade bombs that had been hidden on Bridgefoot Street and also to get supplies. McLoughlin recalled that

> shifting the bombs was no joke. Placed in a wooden box, they weighed nearly half a hundredweight. Balancing it on my shoulder, I made my way through the street. Entering a public house to purchase tea and sugar, I deposited it on the counter. The assistant gave it a scared look; he was one of those that should have been 'out' [as part of the mobilisa-tion for the Rising itself]. I have never seen tea and sugar served so promptly in Ireland.[195]

115

Admittedly, the sight of Daly's men making their arrangements across the river at the Four Courts had terrified the inhabitants.

On his return, McLoughlin had some tea, but also found that Heuston 'became very enthusiastic about my going out again'; he suggested to McLoughlin that his next errand should be to the Heuston family home. Heuston was apparently worried that the house might be raided and incriminating material would be found there. McLoughlin agreed to go and also to deliver a despatch to the GPO on the way back (there was a suggestion that Heuston himself had gone to the GPO, but this seems unlikely).[196]

And so McLoughlin went out again, this time to Fontenoy Street, where Mrs Heuston 'stuffed me with tea and cakes' and, seemingly, he collected more food and ammunition.

Michael Heuston, however, recalled his visit in a slightly different light:

> About two o'clock, a young fellow with a topcoat buttoned tight up on him arrived at home. Mother and Duckie, having heard the firing, which at first they thought was some work going on on the railway, had gone out to see what was on, and the door was opened by Teasie, [Heuston's aunt]
>
> 'I want to get to Seán's room,' he said.

'You can't get to Seán's room. Where is Seán and how do you want to get to his room?'

He produced a pistol and pointed it at her.

'He sent me here and told me to go to his room and get the ammunition there. He gave me his key and said I must get in somehow if you were out.'

He produced the key and Teasie tried it in the door.

'Well, you'll get nothing if you go to his room. You'd better come in and wait till Mrs Heuston comes back. She won't be long.'

He came in.

'Where is Seán?'

'Don't you know we're fighting the soldiers?'

'What? Are you mad? A handful like you to be fighting the soldiers.'

'We're alright. We're expecting the Germans; there'll be 50,000 here by Saturday, or Monday at latest.'

'And where is Seán now?'

'Seán brought us into the Mendicity Institute today at twelve o'clock. We're quite safe; we're in the best place.'

She gave him Jack's dinner.

'That's grand,' said he. He showed her his Fianna uniform under the overcoat.

'If they see this, I'll be shot.'

Mother came in and gave him the ammunition, stuffing it into his pockets.

'Now I have to climb back over the wall into the Mendicity, and I may be shot doing so. I had to shoot a soldier in the lane behind it when coming out. Then a lot of soldiers' wives and people followed me. I led them up a lane and turned round to them took out my pistol and pointed it at them. "Now," I said, "it's your life or mine." A girl fainted and I left them there.' Teasie gave him a Sacred Heart badge as he had not one, and he went off. His name was McLoughlin. He got back alright, for mother afterwards got the latchkey with Jack's things.[197]

Judging by his version of the visit, McLoughlin was prone to exaggeration. Mrs Heuston also gave him some food and he made his way to the GPO, where Connolly told him that the Volunteers in the Mendicity could expect reinforcements arriving at Kingsbridge Station to come their way that night.[198]

In McLoughlin's absence, others had noted what was going on around Usher's Island. Charles MacAuley and some companions were travelling down the quays en route to Leeson St, when they were caught in the crossfire; they took shelter at the north quay wall while troops fired over their heads from the other side of the road. They prudently retraced their steps and took the longer route home.[199] Domhnall Ó Buachalla (a future Governor General of the Irish Free State) had travelled to Dublin from Maynooth on hearing that the Rising had broken out. He cycled down the north quays, where he actually managed to get past the gunfire; by now the soldiers were themselves sheltering at the quay wall.[200] He was only stopped at a Volunteer barricade at the Four Courts. Presumably this happened prior to 4pm, which is when another, larger, column of soldiers arrived on the quays. The Volunteers in the Mendicity fired at them rapidly, concentrating on the front and rear of the column as they did so.[201] By this stage, hundreds of troops had taken over the area on the north quays, from Benburb Street to Queen Street Bridge.[202]

The British made use of the back streets around Smithfield to concentrate a large number of troops on Queen Street. They also brought a machine gun and began to fire at the Mendicity.

> A Volunteer aimed at him [the machine gunner]. Jack told
> him not to, but he fired and probably missed. The gun swept
> the length of the quay.[203]

The Volunteers had no option but to take cover from this onslaught. Heuston may have been concerned that the firing from the Mendicity would attract attention to the Volunteers inside it, but if so, it was too late. According to Stephenson, Heuston

> shouted to us to hold our fire, but in truth all we could do
> was to lie watching the back walls of the room being rid-

dled with bullet holes, and plaster float across the room in a fine grey mist. [204]

When Michael Heuston visited the building after the Rising, he noticed how relatively few bullets had hit the exterior walls, but that the gunfire had been concentrated on the windows and had riddled the rooms inside.[205] These soldiers were hardly inexperienced.

In the midst of the barrage, Heuston crawled across the landing, then he and Stephenson went downstairs, where they took some of the home-made bombs and some candles, and crawled into the room nearest to Queen Street.[206] From there they could seen that the machine gun was providing cover for troops crossing Queen Street Bridge. Heuston lit the candles, both men put the fuses into the flames and Heuston told Stephenson 'don't throw it until they are in the courtyard.' Soon, the first soldier's helmet appeared at the outer wall, but instead of entering the courtyard he jumped across the gate, as did an 'innumerable' number of his colleagues ('how many of these rabbits hopped across that opening I could not tell'). They went towards Watling Street and Stephenson was stunned that 'the expected assault had not materialised.' The soldiers had presumably decided to avoid the Mendicity and continue on to their original destination, giving Heuston and his men a lucky escape as they did so. On a less positive note, however, the fuses of the bombs had not lit. They did not work. Stephenson ruefully consoled himself with the knowledge that they might be heavy enough to knock somebody out. [207]

It had been a very lucky escape. As McLoughlin was still absent, only thirteen men were in the building: they could easily have been overrun. At this stage in the afternoon they could do little but listen to gunfire from elsewhere in the city and clean their weapons, though this noise faded away. Inevitably, doubts began to set in. Pedestrians were moving again on the quays and, above all, the abandoned tram suddenly began to move towards the Four Courts. As far as Stephenson was concerned, 'that tore it. If the tram men were back on the trams and they were on the move again everything must be normal in the city. Daly could not be in the Four Courts. They must have been driven out of the GPO as well. The rebellion must have collapsed.'[208]

Heuston seemed to think the same thing: he 'came into the room to confer with Dick Balfe as to what we should so. He was very puzzled and agreed that it looked as if this was another fiasco.' He began to inquire about possible escape routes, up towards Thomas Street via the Marshallsea Barracks, or Island Street, or Bridgefoot Street. McLoughlin's absence seemed to convince Heuston that the game was up and that there had been 'a complete collapse of the mobilisation, and [this] appeared to help him to decide finally that we had better evacuate.' He instructed his men that it was time to do so. They were told to clean themselves up, leave one at a time, hide their gear and head for home. Stephenson was cleaning himself when he heard a commotion from downstairs: McLoughlin had returned at around 6pm, having made his way back to the Mendicity via Dame Street and Parliament Street, with news of Pearse's reading of the proclamation, the capture of the GPO, the attack on the lancers in O'Connell Street and the fighting around City Hall, some of which he had apparently seen. He also elaborated upon his account with tall tales of the Germans coming up the River Shannon.

Those in the Mendicity were intensely curious to hear what was happening: they were 'put in great spirits' by the news.[209] Pearse and Connolly had apparently been delighted to hear what was happening along the quays. According to Balfe, 'everybody in the GPO thought we would have been wiped out at the time', which may explain why 'we received no message to evacuate.'[210] As Stephenson observed, McLoughlin 'would have made a great minister of propaganda, with his mixture of truth and near lies'; Balfe was apparently more sceptical of his wilder claims. Despite this, McLoughlin's arrival galvanised the small group of Volunteers, who greeted his disclosures with euphoria. But 'we were soon recalled to our senses by a sharp order from Heuston to return to our posts.'[211]

Over the course of the evening the Volunteers pondered what they had heard. Stephenson, a teetotaller, gave the bottle of stout to one of his colleagues, Tom Kelly, who welcomed it as 'manna from heaven'. They settled down for the night. 'At night the Volunteers slept and watched in batches.' [212] Heuston detailed them to sleep in groups of four, fully armed, for three hours at a times. [213] Dublin was silent and dark: neither gas nor electric lighting was working. But later, the Volunteers heard the sounds of 'heavy traffic'; a voice shouted in to the Mendicity that 'soldiers were making their way from the Royal Hospital into James' Street. [214] What Stephenson heard were horses and carts, beginning at Kingsbridge and coming closer (having very likely been transported to Dublin by Heuston's colleagues in the GSWR). This was horse-drawn artillery and as it drew closer Stephenson and the others saw 'the chance of a lifetime'; presumably, the British did not realise that the Mendicity was still occupied. After all, as Balfe recalled, 'on Monday night the British posted sentries right under us and shouted out 'one o'clock; two o'clock, all well!' and so on. These were withdrawn at daybreak.' [215] The Volunteers readied themselves to rush downstairs and ambush the guns. But Heuston intervened

he ordered us to hold our fire – under no circumstances was a shot to be fired – and to go back to our positions and keep quiet. With a deafening clatter the artillery teams drew abreast with the Mendicity, passed it unharmed and with a scramble of hooves wheeled sharply into Bridgefoot Street and were gone. We listened to the sounds dying out as they went up Bridgefoot Street towards Thomas Street. As the noise died down, the hope that Daly, as they passed the Four Courts, would do the job, died out. It is a great tribute to the confidence the small garrison had in Heuston's ability that this decision was accepted without question or grumbling. So from that until daybreak the sleepless watch at the windows was continued.[216]

It seems unusual that Heuston told them not to fire, considering why they were there in the first place. But equally, Heuston and his men were supposed to have abandoned the Mendicity Institution on Monday afternoon; in the circumstances, with large numbers of troops entering the city, it may have been prudent not to have drawn attention to themselves in the darkness.

Early on Tuesday morning, Heuston took stock of their circumstances. He asked Balfe about the possibility of making sandbags from a small garden patch at the back of the building and continued to quiz Stephenson about possible escape routes towards Thomas Street. But 'it was now evident that he was considering the possibility of holding onto his position, although his orders were to hold it for three hours.'[217] Heuston examined the side gates of the Mendicity and the buildings behind that overlooked much of the courtyard and the upper stories, before announcing that he was going to 'partially disobey his orders and try to hold out longer.' The ubiquitous McLoughlin was despatched to the GPO once again, leaving via Bridgefoot Street and taking the route by which he had returned the previous day. Things were quiet enough to allow him to stop off for a cup of tea with Daly at the Father Mathew Hall on Church Street.[218]

On Tuesday the quays were initially empty and silent, devoid of both soldiers and 'highly unintelligent inquisitive civilians'.[219] What the Volunteers in the Mendicity did hear, however, was the faint sound of hammering coming from the direction of Watling Street. They realised that troops were breaking through the walls of houses, presumably under the impression that they were occupied by the Volunteers. The British had bypassed the Mendicity, though the Volunteers remained aware that sooner or later they might reach the Watling Street side of the building. Apart from this, those inside the building remained unmolested.[220] But this did not last. Balfe stated that the British began to use machine guns from the other side of the river on Tuesday and by this time troops were also located in Benburb Lane. More troops came down from the Royal Barracks and were fired upon again: two apparently got across the river, but the rest retreated up Queen Street before being driven out by 'our troops'.[221] According to Brennan, firing continued all day from Queen Street Bridge and Arran Quay, though it petered out in the evening. He claimed that the Four Courts Garrison burned a number of houses at the corner of Bridge Street in order to help the Mendicity.[222] Equally, Michael Heuston recorded that the soldiers bombed a number of houses as they tried to get closer to the building.[223]

McLoughlin was absent as this was going on. When he got to the GPO, Connolly and Pearse 'were astonished that the Mendicity still held out and agreed it would be worthwhile to reinforce the garrison', so they decided to send reinforcements. The men in question turned out to be Volunteers from around Swords in North County Dublin, under Richard Coleman. McLoughlin provided them with directions. According to James Crenigan,

> about 5 or 6pm ten of us were fell in and preceded by a guide who was a Dublin man. We moved out and down Henry Street and through a number of back streets which I did not know, and also through a lot of back yards. We crossed the Liffey at the bridge west of Capel Street Bridge and thence by further back streets eventually arrived through the back way into the Mendicity Institute. From the time we left the GPO were were nearly always under fire but we got there without any casualties.[224]

They crossed Queen Street bridge and went up Bridgefoot Street. They jumped over the walls of the houses to the east, bringing a British soldier captive as they did so: one of the Volunteers in the Mendicity nearly shot the prisoner until he realised that they were not being attacked: it was merely the reinforcements that had been despatched to the Mendicity.[225] They arrived some thirty minutes after McLoughlin, who had obtained some additional food in the GPO: Heuston was pleasantly surprised at their arrival, which proved to be fortuitous.[226] Michael Heuston later recorded some of what had happened in McLoughlin's absence:

> In the Mendicity, two deserted. One, Jack's lieutenant, [Liam Murnane], took off his uniform and went home, saying 'it's murder to stay here.' The Volunteers in many places were used to [taking] off their uniforms, put on their ordinary clothes and go home at night, but this was not done at the Mendicity. Staines says he left not his uniform but his Lee Enfield rifle, which he (Staines) got afterwards. Jack told the men to shoot him if they saw him again. He was extremely disappointed about him. He said it was the last man he expected it of. The other deserter was named Byrne.[227]

Murnane was apparently ostracised by his colleagues when they later encountered him as an internee in Frongoch.[228]

According to one of the new arrivals, Thomas Peppard, 'all was quiet when we got there ... The place had been barricaded but not very effectively.' Matters were not helped by the poor weapons of the reinforcements: they were armed with single-barrelled shotguns, which would only be effective at close quarters. Peppard also noted, ruefully, that while the Mendicity commanded a good position facing the Liffey, its rear was overshadowed by the towers of the massive

Guinness complex.[229] All in all, this did not bode well. In McLoughlin's absence, Stephenson had also taken stock of their situation and also concluded that it wasn't good:

> The inspection had made it clear, by revealing our weaknesses that to put it mildly, our position was not a healthy one. The large double wooden gate at the back into Island Street was not barricaded, because there was nothing to use as a barricade, to stem a rush once the gate was blown in. Immediately in front on Usher's Island there was complete cover for bombing parties to take up positions on each side right under the five foot stone wall in front, and lob their bombs in through the open sashes devoid of the wire mesh protection against this form of attack. Although the Mendicity was completely detached from the houses on both sides, there was again perfect cover for similar parties provided by the six foot high stone walls of the side passages leading to the rear of the building. Only the width of the river and the two quays separated us from the houses right opposite where an occupying force could establish almost point blank domination of the front of our own position. The second attack of the evening had shown how easily this could be done with one machine gun. The placing of the Mendicity in relation to the terrace of houses east and west of it presented an ideal opportunity for making it untenable in the front with a minimum of loss. The front of the building we were holding was set back some thirty-six feet

behind the back of the houses on either side. Once occupied by the British it was only a matter of punching loop-
holes in the side walls of each houses and the second and
top floors were within fifteen feet range of the British fire
on the east side and thirty feet on the west side. But such
was the confidence inspired in us by Heuston that these
observations did not disturb us.[230]

The sound of gunfire from elsewhere in the city could
be heard as the new arrivals were dispersed throughout the
building by Heuston, who refused to believe the captured
soldier's claim that he was a deserter intent on joining the
rebellion and imprisoned him in an upstairs room.[231] He was
apparently 'intoxicated', having been found hiding under a
cart.[232] As James Crenigan, who had arrived with Peppard
and the others recalled,

> we were posted at the windows on both floors, front and
> back. There was practically no protection in the windows
> and certainly no sand-bags. Sniping and volley firing was
> continous at British troops on the North Quays and coming
> from the Royal Barracks. There was no relief – you just
> slept at your post when you got a chance, and food was usu-
> ally brought to us at the window. Food consisted of tinned
> meat, tinned fish, tea, bread and butter. Bread seemed to be
> very scarce. As well as I can remember there were about
> forty men in this garrison. Commandant Heuston was in

command here. Firing continued throughout the night.'[233]

Stephenson was exhausted and eventually dozed off. He awoke after dark, but Heuston instructed that he be let sleep for as long as he wanted. On returning to his position by the window, he noticed that the hammering and gunfire had all ceased.[234] According to Michael Heuston,

on Tuesday night, a detachment of about four hundred soldiers passed under the Mendicity. Jack would not let his men fire, as the soldiers had artillery. As they were going by, they heard an officer say, 'what about this place?'

'We'll see to this afterwards' was the reply. They could not pass the barricade and had to turn up the lane beside the Mendicity.[235]

Tuesday night had been quiet, but on Wednesday morning it was obvious that the supplies of food in the Mendicity were low: an issue exacerbated by the additional numbers who had arrived on Tuesday. Heuston – 'now quite cheerful, very confident' – ordered McLoughlin and Stephenson to go to the GPO to get extra food and to keep Connolly informed. Heuston told them to go out by the back entrance, and went out into Island Street himself to find it deserted. The two Volunteers slipped out and Heuston shut the gate behind them.

As they moved towards Bridgefoot Street the soldiers at

Watling Street opened fire on them: they ran across the street and a dip in the road took them out of the line of fire. As they made their way to Bridge Street an irate woman called out at them, 'There is two of them. The curse of God on you, it's out in Flanders you should be, you bastards.'

McLoughlin and Stephenson proceeded up Church Street and arrived at the GPO via North King Street, Capel Street and Henry Street. Connolly was delighted to hear their news and insisted on sending back a congratulatory message. They also spoke to Michael Staines, whose brother Liam was in the Mendicity and who was relieved to hear that he was unharmed.[236] But in the meantime, the final British attack on the small outpost had come.

Troops had been boring through the neighbouring buildings and by Wednesday morning had apparently reached the back of the Mendicity; in doing so, they had cut it off.[237] The nearby houses were evacuated and the Mendicity was surrounded by troops on the quays, Bridgefoot Street, Bonham Street, and Watling Street. Brennan recalled that

> the British opened an attack from all sides; close quarter encounters were frequent; I remember firing at a soldier only twenty feet away. Machine-gun fire and rifle fire kept up a constant battering on our position. Heuston constantly visited the posts to cheer up the men. But he knew the position was hopeless.[238]

There was originally supposed to have been a detachment of Volunteers in the building behind the Mendicity, 'which was the real danger area.' But if they had ever been there they were gone, and the building had been left vulnerable from the rear.[239] Michael Heuston later pieced together what had happened just before his brother was forced to surrender:

> The soldiers had come round the back streets to the bridge near the city and had a machine gun mounted on it. They had another on the roof of the Phoenix Picture Palace. Snipers were on the roofs of the houses opposite, especially the Phoenix; others were under the quay walls on the opposite side. There were soldiers with very good shots this time and it was impossible to come near the windows without great danger, so Jack ordered his men to keep low. The man who lived in the place said he passed down several times but could see no one at the windows. Balfe and Staines were in the living room and had barricaded the windows as best the could with the furniture. No one was in the next rooms. Two Swords men were in the bathrooms on the ground floor watching the back of the place. Jack was near the door with a grenade in his hand, ready to light it and throw it among the soldiers if they attempted to rush in. These grenades were manufactured at Liberty Hall and consisted of tin cans filled with dynamite, gelignite, etc, with an iron top fitted on with a bolt and a time fuse burning for six of eight seconds attached. The bulk of the Volunteers were on the

ground floor. Soldiers were posted at both ends of the lane behind the building.[240]

By noon troops had crawled along the quay to the outer wall of the Mendicity and began to fling grenades in.[241] Balfe and Liam Staines were badly wounded when they tried to throw them back; Staines received head injuries that were dressed by Heuston, while Balfe was immobilised.

According to Michael Heuston,

> Soldiers then, covered by the fire from across the river, came along from the left under the shelter of the walls in front and began to throw in the grenades. There were no shutters on the windows; had there been, the grenades must largely have failed. One fell between the two Swords men and killed them, probably instantly, one certainly.
>
> Another hit Staines, who was standing near the door of the room. The lower half of the door was blown away and a large hole made right through the floor. He was stunned for a instant but recovered almost immediately. Balfe said he was struck by the same grenade, though he was standing at the window, at the opposite side of the room, trying to get a shot at the soldiers throwing the grenades. The men called on Jack to surrender.[242]

But the end was near. The Volunteers were without food and ammunition and, after consulting them, Heuston decided to surrender.

> Jack threw out a white sheet, but the soldiers continued
> firing. He then sent out the captive soldier, but they sent
> him back, saying they wanted a Volunteer. Jack came to the
> door, put out the white flag and called out: 'Do you rec-
> ognise the white flag?' They said 'yes', but he seems not to
> have heard and repeated the question. 'Yes', they said, 'come
> out.'[243]

They destroyed as much incriminating material as was
possible before emerging towards the back gate with a white
sheet as a flag. At this point, a sniper in the brewery behind
the Mendicity shot dead Peter Wilson (whether by accident
or design is unclear) from Swords, one of the reinforcements
who had arrived the day before. Soldiers were lying on Island
Street, with their rifles at the ready.[244]

According to his brother Michael, Seán Heuston,

> came out then and surrendered … A quarter of an hour
> had not elapsed since the soldiers first got in the grenades.
> Jack then went back and, helping Staines on one side while
> someone else supported him on the other, came out fol-
> lowed by the rest. The girl who lives there says that if she
> had been in it she could have got them out by some way
> she knew.[245]

Brennan recalled that 'we were compelled to walk to the

Royal Barracks with our hands raised, held behind our heads. The British were infuriated when they saw the pigmy force of twenty three men who had given them such a stiff battle and caused them so many casualties.'[246]

Balfe had been left behind due to his injuries. The troops broke in later that day and he was found by a British officer and a Dublin Fusilier and 'while they were deciding to use a bayonet or a bullet an officer of the RAMC came in and claimed me as his prisoner saying there had been enough of this dirty work.'[247]

The fighting in the area around the Mendicity Institution had been sporadic and of short duration, but of great intensity; 'deafening firing', as one witness recalled.[248] There had also been scope for the surreal: at one point while it was going on, 'a street musician came along, and from some secure cover close to the Mendicity itself, commenced to play an Irish tune. The effect was so extraordinary upon all of us that, with the exception of the fight going on at the Mendicity, action in our vicinity almost ceased.'[249] By Wednesday afternoon, 'the fight going on at the Mendicity' had also ceased.

By this time, McLoughlin and Stephenson had made their way from the GPO back to the quays through Parnell Street, Bolton Street and North King Street. As they did so, they had been surprised to see civilians milling about. When they got to Church Street Bridge they went into a sweet shop that was being used as an outpost and from their vantage point saw a British sentry outside the Mendicity Institution.

Here is where accounts differ. McLoughlin claimed to have heard heavy fighting as they approached Church Street, and to have witnessed the attack on the building.[250] Stephenson did not, but he recalled his shock: he knew that Heuston fully intended to hold out as long as he could, so if the building was captured he and the others were either dead or imprisoned. McLoughlin told Stephenson to wait while he slipped out to investigate.[251] He returned none the wiser; nobody had seen any frontal attack on the Mendicity. But McLoughlin went out again, and having spoken to 'a Miss Martin who lived in the Mendicity', he heard that Heuston and the others were seen being marched towards the Royal Barracks, and that Balfe and Staines were 'stretcher cases'. He also saw that the Tommies were being welcomed with bread and butter and tea on Church Street, and after being spotted he beat a hasty retreat.[252] According to Stephenson,

> We tried to find consolation as we thought of how long Heuston had held out against such superior numbers and that it was ridiculous to think that he could have beaten off such forces. There was nothing to be ashamed of in losing such a scrap, particularly under such adverse conditions.[253]

Dejected, McLoughlin and Stephenson made their way

back towards the Four Courts, and thence to the GPO.

It had become extremely dangerous to attempt to approach the Mendicity during the fighting, but after its capture the troops were able to move along the quays without hindrance; concrete proof that, as far as those who had occupied the building were concerned, their Easter Rising was over.[254]

Chapter 8

Capture and Courtmartial

Heuston and his men were marched across the river and were detained in Arbour Hill prison, a stern limestone edifice built in the 1840s as a military prison. They were confined in the gymnasium, which was soon filled with prisoners. Ironically, it was located directly behind the Royal Barracks, where the troops that Heuston's men fired at on Easter Monday had come from. While in captivity, Heuston encountered a former colleague from the GSWR: Jack Mount, who worked in the same office as him but had joined the British army; he was stationed in the barracks just across the river from where he and Heuston had worked. On Easter Monday Mount and his colleagues had been despatched to Dublin Castle; he and a number of others went via Watling Street and Frederick Street and saw fighting around Christ Church, where they lost some of their number. He remained in the Castle for the rest of the week and only returned to the Royal Barracks on Sunday. Mount later told

Michael Heuston that, on hearing that Seán was in captivity, he had been willing to let his old colleague slip away. But an officer made it clear that this was unacceptable, 'for the reason that one of their officers, [Neilan], had been killed by Jack's group. Mount argued that it was impossible to know whether this was so, but the others replied that there was no other that could have been responsible.' It was made quite clear to Mount that he would be arrested if he tried to help Heuston, so he told his commanding officer that,

> if any question arose of his serving on a court as a junior officer he would object, to which the officer replied that if he was asked for a member for the court he would be obliged to name Mount. Mount said that in that case he would simply have to say 'not guilty' to each case. The matter did not arise.[255]

Heuston was detained in Arbour Hill for a week, sleeping on the floor of the gym. He had been searched on his arrival and his personal effects – a watch, money and, crucially, some papers – were taken from him. Then, 'on the morning of Thursday, 4 May, he was awakened at three o'clock' and the charge against him read out – that he:

> Did an act [sic], to wit, did take part in an armed rebellion and the waging of war against His Majesty the King, such act being prejudicial to the Defence of the Realm, and being committed with the intention and purpose of

assisting the enemy.[256]

Heuston was then transferred to Richmond Barracks in Inchicore to stand trial on the same day. He does not seem to have been subject to the form of selection that so many other prisoners underwent in Richmond Barracks, as detectives from the DMP's G-Division went through the ranks of prisoners to winnow out leading suspects. Heuston had, after all, been caught red-handed. He later told his brother Michael that the trial lasted about twenty minutes and Heuston – prisoner number forty-six – was one of four prisoners tried. The others were W. O'Dea, P. Kelly and James Crenigan. All had been charged with the same offence and were being prosecuted under the wartime Defence of the Realm Act. Implicit within the charge was the lurking shadow of the Great War, but the act had not anticipated an armed rebellion breaking out within the United Kingdom; hence the nature of the charge itself. Like all of those prosecuted after the Rising, the four men were tried in camera by a relatively perfunctory Field General Court Martial, consisting of Brigadier Ernest Maconchy as presiding officer, along with Lt. Col. A.M. Bent of the Royal Munster Fusiliers and Major F.W. Woodward of the Lancashire Regiment.[257] Perhaps ironically, Maconchy was Irish, having been born in Longford, and was uneasy with the task he was now obliged to fulfil.[258]

Unsurprisingly, all four defendants pleaded not guilty.

Heuston kept a copy of the charge in his own handwriting, along with a note that provided his perspective on what he had been involved in.

> War commenced Monday, April [24] 1916 at noon, surrendered to vastly superior numbers and armaments Wednesday April 26. Lodged Arbour Hill Detention B[arracks] until Thursday May 4th. [?] at Richmond Barracks May 4th. Lodged in Kilmainham Prison May 4th.[259]

Jack Mount did not testify, but two other members of the Royal Dublin Fusiliers did. The first was Captain A.W. MacDermot of the 7th battalion, who stated that

> On the 26th April I was present when the Mendicity Institution was taken by assault by a party of the 10th Battalion Royal Dublin Fusiliers.
>
> Twenty-three men surrendered on that occasion. I identify the four prisoners J.J. Heuston, W. O'Dea, P. Kelly and J. Crenigan as having been in the body of men who surrendered.
>
> They left their arms except their revolvers in the Mendicity Institute when they surrendered. Some of them still wore revolvers.
>
> One officer of the 70th Royal Dublin Fusiliers was killed and nine men wounded by fire from this Institute on the 24th April.

I searched the building when they surrendered. I found several rifles several thousand rounds of ammunition for both revolvers and rifles (.303).

I found six or seven bombs charged and with fuses in them ready for use.

I found the following papers.

An order signed by James Connolly, one of the signatories to the Irish Republic Proclamation, directing 'Captain Houston' [sic] to 'seize the Mendicity at all costs'. It was dated the 24th April 1916.

James Connolly signed as 'Commandant General Dublin Division'.

Also papers detailing men for various duties in the Mendicity Institute. All these papers are headed 'Army of the Irish Republic'.

Also two message books signed by Heuston 'Capt'.

One contains copies of messages sent to 'Commandant General Connolly' giving particulars of the situation in the Institute.

The other message book contains copies of messages commencing on the 22nd April two days before the outbreak. One message contains a reference to Macdonagh [sic] who is stated to have just left Heuston.

Another is a message to 'all members of D Company 1st Battalion' stating that the parade for the 23rd is cancelled and all rumours are to be ignored.

Another message dated the 23rd states 'I hope we will be able to do better next time.'

The papers in question were presented to the court and when questioned MacDermot confirmed that 'Heuston commanded the party of men who surrendered'.

The court-martial continued with the calling of a second witness for the prosecution immediately after the first: Lt. W.P. Connolly of the Royal Dublin Fusiliers, who testified that:

I was present when twenty-three men surrendered on the 26th April at the Mendicity Institute.

I identify the four prisoners before the court as being amongst them.

The leader was J.J. Heuston.

I was present when the troops were fired on from the Mendicity Institute on the 24th April, when Lt G.A. Neilan was killed and six men wounded to my knowledge.

Heuston was without a coat when he surrendered and also had no hat on. He was not in the uniform of the Irish Volunteers.

I was present when the building was searched and found arms and ammunition in it and also the documents now before the court.

Heuston questioned him, presumably about the incriminating papers, and Lt. Connolly's response was that 'I cannot say exactly where I found the message books but they were in the building'. The presiding officers seem to have followed this up with a question about the weapons that were found. Lt. Connolly informed them that 'among the arms were some old German Mausers', presumably some of the Howth Mausers, and 'among the ammunition there were two cardboard boxes of "Spange" German ammunition.'

Finally, the four prisoners were given a chance to defend themselves in a somewhat perfunctory manner. O'Dea, Kelly and Crenigan all claimed that they had turned up on Easter Monday for their standard route marches and manoeuvres and had known nothing of the planned rebellion. O'Dea added that he had been told that the best equipped company would get a prize, Kelly that he had not fired any shots and Crenigan that he was sixteen years old. Heuston, however, put forth a novel, if tenuous, defence:

> The message in the notebook produced saying, 'I hope we will be able to do better next time' is not mine. The order from Connolly addressed to 'Captain Houston' is not addressed to me as my name is 'Heuston'. I had no intimation of the nature of the charge against me until this morning.

Connolly had, presumably, used the Scottish spelling of the name that he naturally would have been more familiar with.[260] Heuston effectively staked his life on a single letter – and lost. He, O'Dea and Kelly were all found guilty and sentenced to death. Crenigan's plea seems to have succeeded: he received 'two years imprisonment with hard labour, recommended to mercy on account of his youth.' Both O'Dea and Kelly had their sentences commuted to three years each, on account of their having been 'misled'. But Heuston's remained unchanged and he was transferred to Kilmainham. Within a matter of days, the sentence had been confirmed and he was dead.

• • • • •

Chapter 9:

From Sentence to Execution

After his court-martial in Richmond Barracks, Heuston was detained in Kilmainham to await the confirmation of the sentence. It came on the following Sunday, 7 May. Éamonn Ceannt, Con Colbert, Heuston and Michael Mallin were seen by some of their fellow prisoners in the front row at Sunday mass in the prison chapel. Annie O'Brien and Lily Curran, two member of Cumann na mBan who had been held in Kilmainham, recalled that:

> They were the only ones to receive Holy Communion, which we thought significant. That affected us all …We craned our necks to try to see more, but the wardresses pulled us back. When the Volunteer prisoners were leaving the church those four were the last to leave and they looked up at us and we waved down to Con Colbert, who waved his hand in reply shaking his head up and down as if in farewell. They evidently knew what their fate would be. They were all four executed next morning.[261]

As it turns out, at that point they did not know what their fate would be. The sentences of death were only confirmed by the newly-installed military governor, General Sir John Maxwell, later on Sunday evening. Heuston told his brother that,

> the day of the trial – Thursday – we got nothing officially from half-seven in the morning till half-nine the next morning. But that was nothing to the mental anguish. That was much worse, not knowing what was coming. And then I was by myself. I never left this cell since Thursday. In Arbour Hill I had been with the others. When I heard nothing on Friday, I thought it would be all right and so did Fr [Albert] and I was just thinking it would be all right when I got word tonight.[262]

Now that he was under no illusion about his imminent fate, Heuston wrote to his brother in Tallaght, and to his mother, his sister Teresa and his aunt Teresa McDonald in Fontenoy Street, requesting that they come to see him. His other sister, Mary, was a Dominican nun in Galway; he knew he would not see her, so he composed a lengthy and revealing last letter to her instead:

> My dearest Mary,
>
> Before this note reaches you I shall have fallen as a soldier

in the cause of Irish freedom. I write to you as a last farewell in this world, and rely on you to pray fervently and to get the prayers of the whole community for the repose of my soul. I go, I trust, to meet poor Brigid [his other aunt] above and am quite prepared for the journey. The priest was with me and I received Holy Communion this morning. It was only this evening that the finding of the court martial was conveyed to me.

Poor Mother will miss me but I feel that with God's help she will manage to pull along. You know the Irish proverb: 'God's help is nearer than the door.' The agony of the past few days has been intense, but I now feel resigned to God's holy will. I might have fallen in action as many have done and been less well prepared for the journey before me. Do not blame me for the part I have taken. As a soldier I merely carried out the orders of my superiors who should have been in a position to know what was best in Ireland's interest. Let there be no talk of foolish enterprise. I have no vain regrets. Think of the thousands of Irishmen who fell fighting under another flag at the Dardanelles, attempting to do what England's experts now admit was an absolute impossibility.

If you really love me teach the children in your class the history of their own land, and teach them that the cause of Caitlín Ní Uallacháin never dies. Ireland shall be free from the centre to the sea as soon as the people of Ireland believe in the necessity for Ireland's freedom and are prepared to make the necessary sacrifices to obtain it. Ireland cannot be freed by strong resolutions or votes of confidence, however unanimous.

It may be that the struggle we have made will lend strength to Ireland's claim for representation at the great peace conference when the map of Europe is being redrawn. Let us pray that Ireland will benefit from it ultimately.

Let you do your share by teaching Ireland's history as it should be taught. Mary, pray for me and get everybody to pray for me.

Your loving brother,

Jack.[263]

The fact that Heuston borrowed a quote from 'The Shan van Vocht', a ballad about the 1798 rebellion, immediately after telling his sister to keep teaching the history of Ireland is a very strong hint as to what aspect of that history he was talking about. Yet his comments on the war display an obvious awareness of contemporary events. His attempt to justify the Rising with reference to the Gallipoli campaign is striking, given that the events of 1916 have often been dismissed for their supposed irrationality. But thousands of Heuston's contemporaries, from both Dublin and the rest of Ireland, were killed or wounded when the 10th (Irish) Division landed at Suvla Bay the year before; in that light, one can understand his desire that there be 'no talk of foolish enterprise'.

It might be worth pausing to remember that Heuston's death sentence had been confirmed by General Maxwell in his capacity as the new military governor of Ireland. Maxwell, however, had not been the first choice for this job. The original choice had been another general, Sir Ian Hamilton, but his appointment was vetoed by the Imperial General Staff due to his association with the Gallipoli campaign. The Irish losses in the Dardanelles had left a bitter legacy and Hamilton was tarred with it. It was felt that his appointment would add insult to injury; it was ironic, in the light of Heuston's comment about the Dardanelles, that Maxwell had been chosen precisely because he was not tainted by one of the more notorious incidents of the war.[264] As for what might follow the war, Heuston's letter was somewhat prescient. The hope that Ireland might get a place at a post-war peace conference was a sentiment shared by Tom Clarke, and became a key objective of the rejuvenated Sinn Féin in the years after 1916. Perhaps the Rising was foolhardy, but Heuston was no fool.

Nor was he oblivious to the effect his death might have on those closest to him. He wrote to one of his superiors in the GSWR, explaining what happened as best he could and imploring him to make some provision for his mother's maintenance:

Dear Mr Walsh,

Before this note reaches you I shall have said farewell to this vale of tears and have departed for what I trust will prove a much better world. I take this last opportunity of thanking you and all my railway friends for the kindness of the past years. I ask all to forgive me for any offences which I may have committed against them and I ask all to pray fervently for the repose of my soul. Whatever I have done I have done as a soldier of Ireland in what I believed to be my country's interests. I have thank God no vain regrets. After all it is much better to be a corpse than a coward.

Won't you as a last favour see that my mother gets whatever assistance you can give in obtaining whatever salary is due to me and whatever regard is due from the superannuation fund? She will stand badly in need of it all.

Gratefully yours,

J.J. Heuston.[265]

That evening, the commandant of the jail had sent a car to Heuston's family home at 20 Fontenoy Street to collect his mother, his aunt and his sister. They travelled to Kilmainham on what was a rainy night, passing through British checkpoints with ease; their driver responded to questions from soldiers who had flagged them down with what Heuston's sister described as the 'cryptic' term 'Kings' messenger!'[266] One of his cousins, Lil, had been present in the house and insisted on accompanying them. This caused some confusion, but she was eventually admitted.

Heuston's brother Michael, however, had arrived at the jail about an hour beforehand and was already in the cell, talking to his doomed brother. Michael left an extraordinarily detailed, almost novelistic account of the final conversation he and his family had with Seán, and all the direct speech that follows is taken directly from it. Conversation that eventually turned to the events that Seán had been involved in. Perhaps understandably, given his vocation, Michael asked what was perhaps the most relevent question of all:

'Did you kill any yourself?'

'No. I had only my automatic pistols and they would not carry. They produced it at the trial that two officers were killed and nine soldiers wounded at the first volley. After that we had not much more fighting till the Wednesday. They came at us with grenades. They were bringing the place down on us and we had to surrender. If you go round there some time, you'll find plenty [of] traces of the fight. I went out with the white flag myself, for I had heard that in another place a man with the white flag had been shot. They told me we had no chance and it was better for us to surrender.'

(Seán seems to have been economical with the truth: Staines later confirmed to Michael that his elder brother

only had his pistols, but that he also 'took up a rifle sometimes and had a shot, too.')

'How many had you with you?' asked Michael.

'I surrendered with twenty-three. Two had been killed,
two got away with despatches, and two deserted. Do you
know Balfe? You must have met him with me sometime.
Perhaps not. He was killed, poor fellow. One of those that
deserted was my lieutenant. I would never have expected it
from him. I trusted him more than the rest. He left his uniform behind him and went away. I heard since that he was
arrested and is in prison.'

Apparently, 'Jack was rather knocked up about Balfe' – at
this stage he did not know that Balfe had, in fact, survived
– and 'he took the desertion of the lieutenant very hard
indeed.'

Heuston soon came, ruefully, to what he felt was the reason
for the death sentence: 'In the excitement of the surrender-
ing, getting out the wounded and the dead, I forgot to burn
the orders from Connolly and they got them on me. They
had them at the trial and it was that did for me.'

He continued. 'I was in Arbour Hill for a week, then on
Thursday I was taken to Richmond Barracks for the trial and
then sent here. When I heard nothing on Friday, I thought it
was all right, and so did Fr Aloysius [Albert].'

'What kind was the trial?' asked Michael. 'Did it last long?'

'About twenty minutes. The officers were all dreadfully

153

vexed because we killed so many soldiers, especially the two officers.'

'About how many soldiers did you kill?'

'I don't know, but we killed a lot. They had the orders from Connolly, but I think they must have got something else too, I don't know what. We were allowed no one to defend us. We were not let open our mouths. We were condemned beforehand and it was only a question of fixing the sentences.'

'Were you on any of their councils?'

'No.'

'Or committees or anything of that sort?'

'No.'

'Did you know beforehand that it was coming off?'

'I had strong suspicions for about a week before, as we were moving a lot of stuff everywhere. We moved a whole cartload from a house in Prussia Street on Good Friday. I was almost certain from that on but got no definite order till Easter Monday morning. We were all in the hall, in Blackhall Lane, guarding dynamite on Easter Sunday night.'

'Had you much?'

'Oh, yes, a whole load.'

'There was a lot taken from the de Selby quarries near Tallaght on Holy Saturday night. Was that it?'

'No, this came from somewhere else.'

'They said there was enough taken from the quarries to

blow up the whole city of it were properly used. Was Mac-Neill's order genuine? Many said it was only a blind.'

'Oh, it was genuine. A lot didn't turn up because of it.'

'Do you know anything of Bulmer Hobson? They say the Volunteers put him out of the way because he was a traitor.'

'Oh, that's not true (I forget exactly what he said about him, but I think he didn't know much definitely).'

Perhaps, given Hobson's role in the Fianna and Heuston's own background in the organisation, he wasn't inclined to think unfavourably of him. Michael's questions continued.

'Did they expect help from Germany?'

'I think so.'

'Is it true what the English say about sinking three transports?'

'I don't know, it may be.'

The collapse of communications in Dublin had ensured that rumour ran rife in the city during Easter week; insurgents such as Heuston were also in the dark as to what was happening elsewhere.

'Do you know did the rest of the country rise?' asked Michael.

'I don't think so – except Galway,' replied Seán.

'That was a pity. Did you hear anything about the fighting in the other parts of the city? I heard very little.'

'O'Connell Street is in ruins.' Seán apparently 'said something about seeing who the Huns are now.'

Michael Heuston was not immune to the power of rumour himself and told Seán some of the more outlandish stories he had heard, such as that 'at Beggars Bush a detachment of five hundred soldiers was destroyed and the machine guns taken from them. The Volunteers attacked them with their bayonets and annihilated them [this may have been a rumour derived from the fighting at Mount Street Bridge]. Also, I heard that a large division had marched from the Curragh or somewhere like that and, being tired, lay down to rest in a field at Dolphin's Barn. The Volunteers, hearing of it, came out with machine guns and wiped them out. They say the Volunteers had great shots. Ten of them held a whole regiment of soldiers at bay for two nights at Blacquiere Bridge [in Phibsborough]. They say there is still fighting going on at Ringsend.'

'Is that true about these places?' asked Seán. 'How many soldiers do you think were killed altogether?'

'Some thousands, I think. It is said up to five thousand.'

'Ah, we could have held out much longer only for the artillery. We never expected they would use it on us. It was that beat us. Anyhow, it was an acknowledgement that they had entirely lost the city, for unless they had lost it they would never have blown down their own city. Even so, we could have held out a month longer, but it was no use … What is the opinion of the country about it?'

'I think the people are on the side of the Volunteers,' replied

Michael. 'Certainly England is putting them more and more on their side by the executions. The country is raging about them. They would scarcely have minded so much the execution of those that signed the proclamation but everyone is wild about the execution of those they never heard of before.' Needless to say, Seán Heuston was in the latter category.

'Did you hear that the English had to surrender at Kut?' he asked Michael. 'It is true, is it not?'

'Oh, yes, it's on the papers.'

'I also heard that Verdun has fallen. Is that true?'

'No, I don't think so; there is nothing about it, though it's in a bad way.'

'No, I suppose it was only some rumour.'

Michael recalled that Seán said 'something about the decline of England,' before telling him, 'Michael, when you have the opportunity, teach the history of Ireland – in the right way. Not the history you get in books but the real history. That's what will put the English out of Ireland – the real history.'

Michael 'told him we were doing what we could in Tallaght for the language.'

'Yes,' said Seán, 'teach the history of Ireland when you can.'

'Mary wrote to me at Easter saying she had a visit from a man of the Educational Company. She said he was the Irish element and his name is Daly. He isn't the Daly that was executed?'

'No,' replied Seán. 'Daly who was executed worked at such a place'; not the Educational Company.

'Well,' said Michael, 'England only waited the chance to show what she is.'

'Yes, the first opportunity she gets you can't trust her. They say they have a pit a hundred yards long dug at Arbour Hill and they are going to fill it.'

'How many have been executed already?'

'Eight: Pearse and Willie Pearse, the Major [MacBride] – did you know the Major? – MacDonagh, Daly, Plunkett, Count Plunkett's son, Tom Clarke, Mícheál Ó hAnracháin – he was a clerk at headquarters.'

'MacDonagh had me for English last year at school – at the University. Fr Browne, too knew him at Rockwell.'

They confirmed this with Fr Browne. 'Oh, yes,' he replied, 'MacDonagh was with me in Rockwell.'

Michael mentioned once again that MacDonagh had taught him.

'Is that so?' said Jack. 'How old was he then?'

'He must have been about forty,' said Fr Michael.

'You'd never think it. He looked only about thirty,' said Seán, who was 'quite surprised' at this.

Seán then turned to more pressing matters.

'I was counting up what money mother will have,' he said to Michael. 'I have a list of things I want you to tell mother. I may tell her myself if she comes.' His hope was that his mother might receive the remainder of his salary. 'I have written to Mr Walsh to give the money to mother, for there is the superannuation: that will come to about £30. Stuff – there is a lot of stuff at home which mother had better get out of the way. There is my rifle – a military one – worth £7.10. I bought it for £2.10.'

'How did you get it?' asked Michael.

'From a deserter or someone, you know.' Presumably this was the rifle he and Stephenson had bought from the young soldier on Usher's Quay. But there were other weapons hidden in the house on Fontenoy Street. 'There is a parcel of eight automatic pistols' each of which was originally worth £20. 'She had better get these things out of the way for the present, and afterwards she can sell them. Of course, she won't be able to sell them yet, but afterwards she will when things quieten down. She won't get all they're worth, but she ought get about £15.'

'How had you all these?' asked Michael.

'I had them to distribute to fellows.'

'Is there any ammunition at home?'

'A few boxes of No 30.'

'What is that?'

'Pistol ammunition; it's no use. I have some money at home, too – £2.10s I made on a rifle. Tell mother to give back 5s to O'Sullivan – it was his subscription towards the camp. There is other Volunteer money at home, too. It belonged to the

Volunteers, but the Volunteers – as a body – no longer exist. I asked Fr [Albert] and he said it would be perfectly alright to use it. I believe the Cumann na mBan have some money for the dependents of the executed, and mother ought to get some of that. Tell her, too, to give my books to anyone who asks for them.'

He then asked Michael if he had anything to tell him.

'I could think of nothing,' recalled Michael. 'I told him I would pray for him and told him not to show any sign of fear to the soldiers in the morning.'

'I'm not afraid, Michael,' said Seán, 'I'm not afraid.'

It was now about 10.40pm. Michael noticed that his brother 'did not look at all so bad. The expression of great anxiety was largely gone and he spoke in a stronger voice.' The conversation with Michael may have relaxed Seán, and if this was the case it happened at a fortuitous time; at this point that the rest of their family arrived.

As they entered Heuston's cell, his sister Teresa recalled that 'one soldier, holding a lighted candle, was in the cell with them. He was young and deeply affected. He was crying.'[267]

His cousin Lil also began to cry.

'Now, Lil,' said Michael, 'this won't do. You're only making it the harder for him.'

Their mother was taken aback by her eldest son's appearance: 'he's only the wreck of the fine, strong young man that went out on Easter Monday morning,' she exclaimed.

According to Michael, Seán 'showed her the list and told her what he had told me already about it', but 'Mother told him she had got rid of all the stuff and that they had burned all kinds of papers and everything to save him.' Given his concern for her future welfare this was hardly what he wanted to know, but she was able to reassure him that Balfe was alive and in hospital, news he was relieved to hear.

According to Michael, 'Mother said she would rather see him gone than in that place for his life. Jack said he was quite satisfied to die. He knew the time of his death and that he might not know otherwise. He might be killed by a car or something in the street any day. He had taken his life in his hands when he went out on Easter Monday and he might have been killed during the fighting. Has asked us to pray for him when he would be gone. Indeed, he asked us repeatedly.'

'I bear no ill will to anyone,' he said. 'If anybody ever did anything against me, I forgive him.'

'Will I get your body?' asked his mother. 'I'd like to bury you with the rest of us in Glasnevin.'

'No', replied Seán, 'we'll all be buried up in Arbour Hill.'

'I'd like to bury you in consecrated ground.'

'Fr [Albert] said he'd bless it – he said he'd bless it a thousand times. He said he'd anoint us after, too. And I'll be with the others – Pearse and Willie Pearse, MacDonagh and Daly and the Major.'

'I'd like to bury you in a habit,' she said. 'The Dominican

habit. I meant that we should all be buried in the Dominican habit. Could it be done, Father?'

'I'm afraid not,' said Browne, 'I think not. If we had known earlier ...'

'Well, all right so.'

'They'll all be buried in their uniforms,' said Heuston, firmly.

'Yes,' said Mrs Heuston, 'and you had no uniform; you couldn't afford it.'

At around 11.30, they said the Rosary.

'Jack knelt at the end of the table facing the door. When we had said ten decades, Fr Michael asked Jack if that were enough. "Oh, no, no, no, go on," he said, and we finished it and then the litany. During the Rosary, the soldier left the candle on the shelf and it fell, leaving us in darkness. When the rosary was finished, it was about 11.40 and we could not stay beyond twelve.'

'Would you like anything?' said Seán to us. 'I have nothing left. They took my watch, the few shillings and everything I had in my pockets at Arbour Hill. A staff officer asked me for something the other day and I gave him my stud – it was the only thing I had left. Do you want anything, Michael?

'It's all right,' was the reply. 'I have your letter.'

'You Lil?'

'Write me something.'

He wrote out a simple message for her: 'Pray for me.

Seaghán MacAodha.'

'I suppose we couldn't get your watch and things?' said his mother.

'I'll write to them,' replied Seán. Apparently, 'he wrote to the Adjutant at Arbour Hill for the things, and also asking him to thank Lieutenant Mount for his kindness. He signed himself J.J. Heuston, Capt, IRA.'

'Will I take it?' said Mrs Heuston.

'Leave it there,' replied Seán. 'It will be all right; it will go officially.' He gave some of the few possessions left to his sister. His mother reminded him of his other sister in Galway, and Browne asked him,

'To whom did you address that letter to your sister?'

'To herself. Wasn't that right?'

'Well, she might get it before learning otherwise. Of course, it would be read before but she might get it unread, and I think it would be better to address it to the Mistress of Novices.'

'Oh, of course. That's the way with me always.' He had to get a pen and paper back from his sister, and as he did so Michael recalled that 'he gave a slight smile – I think the only one.'

'Did you write to father?' asked his mother.

'No, I don't know his address. Kensington Road or something, isn't it?'

'Yes,' she said, 'but better send it to me and I can send it to him.'

Browne told him to kneel down and he gave him his blessing.

'You'll look after Michael?' asked Seán. 'You won't let him cry?'

'No,' Browne assured him, and he also 'promised to say Mass for him and to go see [Seán's] mother the next day.' Then, seeing his concern for his mother, Browne told him

'Don't worry now about mother. She will be all right. We'll see to her.'

Heuston 'seemed relieved' at this. The end was near.

Michael recalled that, as the soldiers came to tell them the visit was at an end, Seán 'was speaking of the treatment they got in prison. They were used like dogs and left without food', and he had been 'pulled out of bed on Thursday morning at three o'clock' and feared that he 'was going to be shot without any trial at all.'

'Well, thank God, that's all over now,' said Seán, 'and I'm satisfied to go. I'm not the first man that has died for Ireland. Don't cry now mother, don't cry. Michael, you won't let mother cry? Pray, pray hard for me.'

And with that, Heuston's family left him and 'the soldiers shut the door, leaving him in the dark.'

'You're not leaving him in the dark?' asked Michael. 'He wants to write.'

'It will be all right,' replied the soldier, 'we'll bring the light back to him.'

The soldier was as good as his word. Heuston's family had left him just after midnight. He had less than four hours to live and he took the opportunity to attend to some final details. He wrote to his mother (to whom all of the letters were to be forwarded), requesting that she take care of a small matter that had slipped his mind:

> My dear mother,
>
> I forgot to mention to you that a refund of 5/s (five shillings) is due to young D. O'Sullivan of Glengarry Parade (I think the number is 33). He paid me the money for the proposed Easter Camp. Give him back the money and ask him to pray and get all the Fianna to pray for me.
>
> Your affectionate son,
>
> Jack.[268]

Heuston was also acutely aware that, as the main breadwinner in his family, his loss would be keenly felt. This seems to be why he wrote a restrained, yet faintly embittered, letter to his estranged father:

> My dear Father,
>
> It is now many years since I have written to you and this will in all probability be the last communication which you will receive from me. I have been sentenced to death for

taking part in the recent Rising [and] the sentence is to be carried out in the morning. I have for years [past] been my mother's main support and now I make this appeal to you from the jaws of death to assist my mother as far as lies in your power.

As for myself I have no vain regrets but go to fall as a true soldier in the cause of freedom. Thousands in the past have fallen in the same way. Many are dying now, and no doubt many will have to fall in the future before final triumph is achieved. As an Irishman won't you breathe an occasional prayer for the repose of all and especially for the soul of your affectionate son, Jack.'[269]

At 1.30am on the morning of 8 May, a military car arrived at the Capuchin Friary on Church Street to bring two of the Friars – Augustine and Albert – to Kilmainham, to minister to the prisoners due for execution that Monday morning. Father Albert was to look after Heuston in his final hours. Having visited Con Colbert and Éamonn Ceannt, he arrived at Heuston's cell at around 3.20am and left a lengthy account of what came next:

He was kneeling beside a small table with his rosary beads in his hand and on the table was a little piece of candle and some letters he had just written to some near relatives and friends. He wore his overcoat, as the morning was extremely cold, and none of these men received those little comforts that are provided for even the greatest criminals while awaiting sentence of death. During the last quarter of an hour we knelt in the cell in complete darkness, as the little piece of candle had burned out; but no word of complaint passed his lips. His one thought was to prepare with all the fervour and earnestness of his soul to meet Our Divine Saviour and His sweet Virgin Mother, to whom he was about to offer up his young life for the freedom and independence of his beloved country. He had been to confession and had received holy communion early that morning, and was not afraid to die. He awaited the end not only with that calmness and fortitude which peace of mind brings to noble souls, but during the last quarter of an hour he spoke of soon meeting again Pádraig Mac Phiaras and the other leaders who had already gone before him.

We said together short acts of faith, hope, contrition and love; we prayed together to St Patrick, St Brigid, St Colmcille and all the saints of Ireland; we said many times that very beautiful ejaculatory prayer: 'Jesus, Mary and Joseph, I give you my heart and my soul.' This appealed very much to him. But though he prayed with such fervour for courage and strength in the ordeal that was at hand, Ireland and his friends were close to his soul. He loved his own unto the end.

In his last message to me he said: 'Remember me to the

boys of the Fianna. Remember me to Mícheál Staines and to his brothers and to all the boys at Blackhall Street.'

At about 3.45am a British sentry knocked at the door of the cell and told us the time was up. We both walked out together, down to the end of the large open space from which a corridor leads to the jail yard. Here his hands were tied behind his back, a cloth over his eyes and a small piece of white paper about four or five inches square, pinned on to his coat over his heart. Just then we saw Father Augustine with Commandant [Michael] Mallin come towards us from the cell where they had been. We were now told to be ready. I had a small cross in my hand, and though blindfolded, Seán bent his head and kissed the crucifix, this was the last thing his lips touched in life. He then whispered to me: 'Father, sure you won't forget to anoint me?' I had told him in his cell I would anoint him when he was shot. We now pro-ceeded towards the yard where the execution was to take place; my left arm was linked in his right, while the British soldier who had handcuffed and blindfolded him walked on his left. As we walked slowly along we repeated most of the prayers that we had been saying in his cell. On our way we passed a group of soldiers. These I afterwards learned were awaiting Commandant Mallin, who was following us. Having reached a second yard I saw there another group of military armed with rifles. Some of these were standing and some sitting or kneeling. A soldier directed Seán and myself to a corner of the yard, a short distance from the outer wall of the prison. Here there was a box (seemingly a soap box) and Seán was told to sit down upon it. He was perfectly calm and said with me for the last time 'My Jesus, mercy'. I scarcely had moved away a few yards when a volley went off, and this noble soldier of Irish freedom fell dead. I rushed over to anoint him. His whole face seemed transformed, and lit up with a grandeur and brightness that I had never before noticed.

Later on his remains and those of the others were conveyed to Arbour Hill military detention barracks, where they were buried in the outer yard, in a trench which holds the mortal remains of Ireland's noblest and bravest sons. Never before did I realise that man could fight so bravely, and die so beautifully and so fearlessly as did the heroes of Easter Week. On the morning of Seán Heuston's death I would have given the world to have been in his place, he died in such a noble and sacred cause, and went forth to meet his Divine Saviour with such grand Christian sentiments of trust, confidence and love. [270]

Seán Heuston appears to have been shot while sitting down. And with that, he passed into history.

Chapter 10:

● ● ● ● ● ●

Doomed Youth?

Heuston's execution was controversial almost as soon as it happened. Madeleine Ffrench-Mullen, who was imprisoned in Kilmainham at the time, observed, after hearing the volleys on the morning of 8 May, that 'it is serious when they begin shooting minor characters like Heuston.'[271] Seán Harling later recalled that

> there were some people you'd never think they'd execute which they did. Like Seán Heuston. He was just an ordinary person, a young lad who was working in Kingsbridge railway station, and he wasn't of any importance, he wasn't like Patrick Pearse. He did command the men in the Mendicity Institute and it's said he did play certain havoc with the soldiers coming out of the barracks and around the quays, but other than that I wouldn't say he was the sort of person who should have been executed. An ordinary army would never have shot the likes of Seán Heuston.[272]

And as Michael Heuston recalled, 'everyone is wild about the executions of those they never heard of.'[273]

In November 1916 the *Gaelic American* published an interview with Heuston's mother, who, on 10 October, had spoken to a journalist, Eileen Moore, at her house on Fontenoy Street.[274] She was described as 'a strong woman – strong mentally and physically', though the journalist noted that Teresa had an unspecified spinal complaint. Mrs Heuston had come to a firm conclusion about the Rising: 'Our men who died fighting or who were shot by the government have done more to further freedom for Ireland than all the parliamentary work of half a century.' As to the question of whether physical force was the right way forward, her view was unambiguous:

Nothing else will accomplish anything … when my boy left me on Easter Monday at 12 o'clock, he had my blessing, and yet both Tessie and I realised poignantly that we might never see him again in life. He was our breadwinner, too. But all considerations were forgotten when Ireland called him.

Was she trying to rationalise the loss of her son by looking to the cause he had served? We cannot know, though her sentiments, as expressed here, were quite republican. Tessie apparently played 'A Nation Once Again' on the piano when they heard that the Rising had begun, 'we were simply delirious with joy. Then we knelt down and prayed that our boy might be spared. We knew the danger he was in.'

But Mrs Heuston had been stunned to hear of the death sentence, 'I didn't believe that they would execute boys. I though imprisonment would have satisfied the government. Everyone was of the same opinion … when I saw my boy in prison I felt proud of him … it was hard on Tessie.'

Mrs Heuston had got upset when he embraced his sister for the last time: 'My boy saw my agitation. He threw his arms around me and said 'You won't cry mother. Promise me you won't fret. What does a few years matter?' … But he was young to die such a cruel death.'

That was not how the British had seen it at the time. General Maxwell had prepared a memorandum on the executed rebels for the benefit of Prime Minister Asquith, in which he gave a somewhat different version of Heuston, who

> was in command of the Mendicity Institute, Usher's Island. One British officer and nine men were killed by the fire from the building which had to be carried [sic] by assault. Twenty-three rebels were captured in it amongst them this man, and large stores of revolver and rifle ammunition and bombs were found. Orders and despatches were also discovered showing that this man was in constant communication with the leaders. In all of these despatches he described himself and was described as Captain.[275]

From a British perspective, this made a clear-cut case. Urban warfare – street fighting – was a relatively new experience for the British military. They had fought rearguard actions in some towns on the Western Front, but what they came up against in Dublin was unprecedented; many of their troops had been inexperienced and the insurgents had exacted a price from them. If Heuston was deemed responsible for some of this, his execution was perhaps inevitable, regardless of Maconchy's reservations.

But there was a certain arbitrariness about the executions: Seán McLoughlin, who died in 1966 after a colourful (if contentious) life as a republican and communist in both Ireland and Britain, attributed his own survival to the actions of an unknown British officer. After the Mendicity Institution had fallen, McLoughlin made his way back to the GPO and was in it when it was finally abandoned. As the republicans from the GPO took refuge in Moore Street, McLoughlin's demeanour and knowledge of the area impressed both Seán MacDiarmada and James Connolly, who insisted that he be given the responsibility of leading a prospective break-out from the area; consequently, McLoughlin was promoted to 'Commandant' and to this end was given a yellow insignia to wear on his tunic. Pearse, however, had reservations about McLoughlin's idea for a suicidal attack on the British barricades at the end of Moore Street and persuaded him to delay it; the eventual surrender ensured that it never took place.

But as McLoughlin was detained in Richmond Barracks, his commandant's insignia caught the eye of a British captain who, on seeing how young McLoughlin was, removed it. In doing so he reduced McLoughlin to the anonymity of the rank and file and very likely saved his life. As McLoughlin later remarked of the unknown officer, 'that man was no enemy'.[276] Did it come down to such a small detail? Quite possibly. But Heuston was not so lucky; his was one of the only courts martial in which documentary evidence had been brought to bear on the proceedings.[277] He told his brother that he was convinced that the court had more evidence than that, but he seems to have been mistaken. If he was executed in part because of his nominal rank, that may have cast a shadow; in the 1960s Michael Heuston published a pamphlet which was largely concerned with making sense of the tangled arrangements that Seán had been involved in and especially with the actual rank he may have held at the time of his death.[278]

At this point it is worth drawing a distinction between Heuston's life and his afterlife. The story of the Easter Rising makes little or no sense when divorced from what it precipitated; it became the catalyst for the remainder of the 'Irish Revolution'. Hence the famous Yeatsian metaphor of the stone troubling the living stream. To assume that 1916, and 1916 alone, triggered the shift in popular support from the cause of Home Rule to that of independence is a gross oversimplification. But as that shift happened, those executed after the Rising were venerated, as their names and lives continued to be harnessed in the service of the republican cause. Soon after his death, a requiem mass had been held for Heuston in the Dominican Church in Dominick Street. It was noted that, as his family emerged,

> they were loudly cheered by a large crowd who had assembled. Members of the throng afterwards sang verses of 'A Nation Once Again', 'Who Fears to Speak of '98', and 'God Save Ireland'. Members of the crowd were observed to be wearing republican badges with mourning tokens.[279]

In early 1917 the Fianna troop in Lismore, County Waterford, were reorganised as the Seán Heuston *Sluagh* and, perhaps more tellingly, in August 1917 a Seán Heuston *Cumann* of Sinn Féin was founded in Carrigaholt, County Clare.[280] His name had acquired a power of its own.

Heuston's life and death also attracted the attention of balladeers:

> Oh! Brave and young Seán Heuston, who died for truth and right
> And gave your life to free our land from Britain's greed and might.[281]

This was not unique to Heuston: all of those executed

after the Rising were venerated as martyrs and not merely for their politics; their religion was also highlighted. As the *Catholic Bulletin* put it soon after the Rising:

> J.J. Heuston, a Dublin boy, comes of a typical Catholic family, his brother being an ecclesiastical student, his sister a nun. Educated by the Christian Brothers, he passed after a brilliant intermediate course, into the service of the Great Southern and Western Railway. The idol of the boy scouts, of whom he was lieutenant, he was sentenced to death by Court-Martial on May 8th. In a letter to a colleague he declared – 'whatever I have done I have done as a soldier of Ireland in what I believe to be my country's best interest. I have, thank God, no vain regrets.' In his final message from his cell, he said, 'Remember me to the boys of the Fianna.' 'The last thing I saw him do', said a Dublin priest, 'was to bend his head and kiss the crucifix as he went out to die.' His last words were, 'My Jesus, mercy!' 'I could eagerly have exchanged places with him at that moment,' said another priest, 'so truly beautiful was his end'. He had a small indulgenced crucifix in his hand when he fell.[282]

Here was Heuston as both Catholic and patriot. His patriotism was highlighted at a memorial ceremony for both him and Colbert, organised by the Fianna and held at Croke Park on 12 May 1918. The souvenir programme told its readers that Heuston's first activities with the Fianna 'commenced

above: Liberty Hall after the fighting. Heuston and the small group under his command assembled here on the morning of 24 April before departing for the Mendicity Institution. Heuston was the only one who knew this to be their destination.

Below left: A barricade of porter barrels provided excellent cover for these British troops in 1916. **Below right:** The shell of the GPO after the Rising. Heuston reported directly to James Connolly and Patrick Pearse in the post office during his occupation of the Mendicity Institution.

Above: The ruins of Henry Street after the Rising: one of the routes taken by messengers and reinforcements shuttling between the GPO and the Mendicity Institution.

Above: Hastily assembled in a Dublin engineering yard, a crude but ingenious armoured personnel carrier for British troops.

Right: Kelly's Gunpowder Office on the corner of O'Connell Street and Bachelors Walk, as viewed from O'Connell Bridge.

Opposite: Troops and prisoners on Ormond Quay: Heuston and his men had been tasked with blocking the movement of troops along the Liffey quays.

Irish Rebellion – May 1916.
A group of Officers with the captured rebel flag.

Opposite top: British officers with the captured 'Irish Republic' flag at the Parnell Monument on O'Connell Street.
Opposite bottom: A car on Mount Street Bridge: another bottleneck that saw heavy fighting as troops attempted to cross it when entering the city.
Left: General Sir John Maxwell: the British military governor who confirmed the executions that followed the Rising. His experience in the Middle East was seen as a useful qualification for his appointment in Ireland.

Right: A plan of a section of Kilmainham Gaol: according to Michael Heuston's recollection, Seán was detained in cell no. 13.

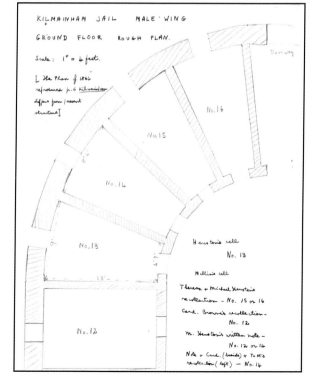

Right: Rev. Michael Heuston at the unveiling of the memorial to his brother Seán in the Phoenix Park, 5 December 1943.

Left: The Capuchin Friar Fr Albert (Thomas Francis Bibby), who ministered to Heuston prior to his execution.

Below: An artist's impression of one the executions in Kilmainham Gaol.

Kilmainham Prison
Sunday.
May 7, 1916

My Dearest M.

I suppose you have been wondering why I did not communicate with you since Easter but the explanation is simple. I have been locked up by his Brittanic Majesty's Government. They have just intimated to me that I am to be executed in the morning. If the rules of the Order allow it. I want you to get permission at once and come in here to see me for the last time in this World. I am prepared to go — I want you to get all said for me.

You will probably be able to come in the motor which takes out this note.

I have sent for Mother. Dickie and Teasie also.

affectionately

Jack.

This page:
Heuston's last letter to his brother Michael.

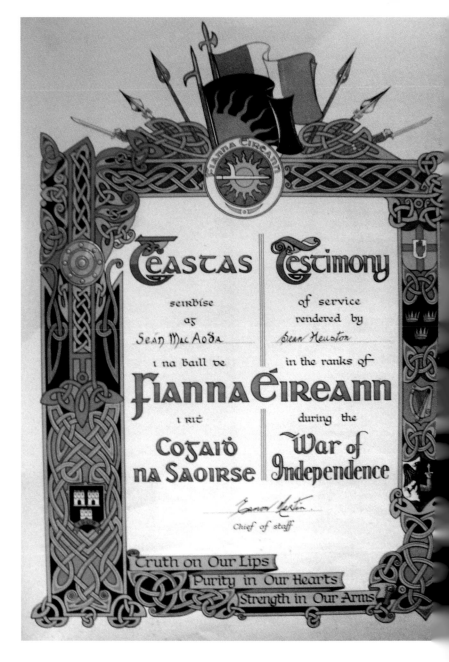

Above: The official testimony of Heuston's service in the Fianna; it was posthumously extended to cover the War of Independence.

while residing in Limerick, where the Fianna *Sluaghte* [sic] grew to such enormity, due largely to his energy and genius ... in supporting motions from the Limerick bodies, he spoke always in Gaelic ... and on all possible occasions avoided English.' But above all, 'the enormous casualty list in the ranks of the enemy who engaged with him in Easter Week bears sufficient testimony to his military genius and bravery ... none were more glad to die for Ireland that Sea-ghan Mac Aodh [sic].'[283]

As late as 1946, on the thirtieth anniversary of the Rising, Heuston and Colbert could be described in terms such as these that brought faith and patriotism together in the most unambiguous manner:

They stood for Irish Ireland at all times and in all places, and were beloved and respected by old and young. Deeply religious as well as intensely Irish, their influence for good was felt wherever they went, and their demeanour and bearing at the hour of death edified even the priests who stood with them to the last. Seán Heuston was in command of a small garrison in the Mendicity Institution ... over that intrepid small body of soldiers and their young leader must have hovered the spirit of Lord Edward Fitzgerald ... the fight at the Mendicity was fierce and terrible while it lasted. Even when the prospects became hopeless the brave little band continued to do battle with far superior and better equipped forces ... the love that had grown and

177

blossomed in his heart during those seven years of service to the Republic of Ireland, strengthened and purified by the true love of God that had been always there, made him stronger a thousand times in that last hour then the Empire that thought it had crushed him and his comrades into dust. Their purpose was pure and unselfish, their cause was holy and just, they had made their peace with God, and through death they had achieved immortality.[284]

The full complexities of Heuston's life are impossible to discern even at this remove, but they were of little relevance to the manner in which his life was used by Republicans prior to 1921 and by the state that came into being thereafter. Millions of young men died across Europe during the Great War and perhaps thirty-five thousand of them were Irish. But in the official culture of the new state, their deaths faded into insignificance beside those of the Republicans whose actions were seen to have led to the foundation of that state. In that regard at least, Seán Heuston was luckier than most.

The Irish dead of the First World War are commemorated at the National War Memorial at Islandbridge. But directly across the River Liffey from it, in the Phoenix Park, Heuston has an individual monument of his own. On 20 March 1938 the Seán Heuston Memorial Committee, which included a number of Heuston's former colleagues (Brennan, Callendar and Stephenson, amongst others) ran an enormously succesful open day at Kilmainham Gaol. The funds raised were earmarked for the eventual memorial to Heuston (sculpted by Laurence Campbell) that was erected in the Phoenix Park on 5 December 1943. Those who attended Kilmainham in March 1938 could have left with a souvenir flyer containing the text of his last letter to his sister.[285] Insofar as Heuston left a political testament, it was this. No doubt his employers in the GSWR would have vehemently disagreed with the sentiments it contained; having been instrumental in moving British troops on the rail network during the Rising, afterwards they took a very stern line towards employees who were suspected of involvement in the Rising.[286] Ironically, as part of the fiftieth anniversary celebrations of the Rising in 1966, King's Bridge over the Liffey was renamed Heuston Bridge, and the old GSWR depot at Kingsbridge was renamed after arguably their most errant employee.

It might be best to end with a question that could usefully be pondered. Given that Heuston is inextricably linked to the fighting around the Mendicity Institution, how effective was the occupation that he presided over? The British military largely bypassed the building as they hastened to more urgent locations and only dealt with it on Wednesday when they began to enter the city to crush the Rising in earnest; they could have done so much earlier had they not decided to avoid it, much to P.J. Stephenson's relief. Heuston told his brother that there was relatively little fighting around the

Mendicity Institution and when Michael Heuston went to visit the building that had sealed his brother's fate he found it battle scarred, but in relatively good condition; perhaps not what one might expect to find had the fighting been of an overwhelming magnitude. Those inside the Mendicity Institution were responsible for the deaths of less than a dozen soldiers, and it seems that at times, they chose not to harass troops who were, quite literally, passing under their windows. But the very presence of Heuston and his men may have served as a deterrent in itself, and the significance of the fighting around the Mendicity Instiution was perhaps more important in principle than in practice. Heuston also told his brother that his task had been not to fight so much as to harass any troops trying to move down the quays. In that sense, his Rising was reasonably succesful. But the realities of Heuston's life and actions were of a different order to the obligation imposed on him in death, as the street fighting around the Mendicity Institution could be magnified out of all proportion to its reality. The facts were best kept out of the way of a good story, for it was the story that came to matter, as Seán Heuston was transformed into one of the youthful faces of Ireland's revolution.

APPENDIX 1:

Kilmainham Gaol Museum, Heuston Collection, 17 LR IC45 10. Bro. John Heuston [Michael Heuston] (St Mary's, Tallaght) to Mary Heuston, 14–16 May 1916. The letter was composed for the benefit of Mary Heuston, but was never sent; it formed the basis of the longer account of Seán Heuston's activities that Michael composed subsequently (see Bureau of Military History (BMH), Contemporary Documents (CD) 309/1. As it stands, the letter is a striking testament to the power of rumour in the aftermath of the Rising. It is reproduced here by permission of Kilmainham Gaol Museum.

Dear Mary,

I intended to write to show you that it was not in a vain and useless rising that Jack gave up his life, but I have heard so many conflicting reports that I think it better to simply enumerate them giving my authorities. You in Galway will find it almost impossible to find out the truth if it is so hard to do so here only six miles or so from the city. Did you get the letter Jack sent you on Sunday night?

Duckie and Teasie have been out this evening and from the account they gave me I feel quite satisfied about Jack – that he died a most beautiful death, having used his life to the utmost. Jack himself on Sunday last told me that he spent Easter Sunday night guarding dynamite. He got his orders to take the Mendicity the next morning and did so. He had no rifle but [had] automatic pistols. He was overturning a motor car, I think, making a barricade when the soldiers came. From the first volley two officers were killed and nine soldiers wounded. This came as evidence at the trial. The court-martial was in a tremendous rage about the officers. He said they had not [seen] very much fighting yet they killed a large number of soldiers. Some people who live on the quays and saw the fight told Fr Egan, our professor at the university, that a lot of soldiers were killed there. They came along jauntily, suspecting nothing and the volunteers opened [up] on them. They fell in all directions. Then they sat down attacking the Mendicity principally with grenades. Some Volunteers were killed, Jack said. On Wednesday Duckie says the soldiers had guns trained on them from the esplanade and Jack's men called on him to surrender. He told me he went himself with the white flag, as he had heard that somewhere else a man negotiating had been shot. The English told him he had no chance and it was better to surrender and he did so. He told me they were bringing the place down on them. I went over the other day but could find no trace of a fight except three bullet marks on the walls and the windows (which seem to have been painted over the glass) all broken not by rifle fire but, as it were, by the volunteers themselves. He surrendered with twenty-three men; two including his lieutenant had deserted, two had been killed and two had gone with despatches. He took it very hard that his lieutenant should have left him. He found afterwards that one of his men [whom] he thought had been killed by a grenade was only badly wounded. Another was wounded by a grenade bursting prematurely in his hand. When he surrendered he forgot to destroy his orders from Connolly. He thought it was because of the large number of soldiers and especially the officers killed that he was shot. He said they also got something else against him, but he did not seem to know what. Possibly and probably it was the work he did for them before the rising. He told me he shot no one himself. They say that 'G' men were the chief witnesses at the trials. He surrendered on Wednesday in Easter Week, was kept in Arbour Hill for eight days, was tried in Richmond barracks on Thursday after low Sunday and was then brought to Kilmainham. He thought it was alright when he heard nothing for three days after [the] trial, then was told on Sunday night. The trial took about twenty minutes and they were allowed no one to defend them. I suppose that is the rule in courts martial. Jack told me that their business in the Mendicity was not so much to fight as to prevent the passage of troops [into] the city, and he seemed rather proud of having done so for two days against tremendous odds.

Fr Albert who attended him told them at home that he died a grand death – not only the death of a hero, but the death of a saint. He even told some of his friends so, who did not know Jack at all.

I suppose you remember Jim Gahan of Wood Quay with whom I used sometimes to go to the [hills]. He has been deported. So has Fergus Kelly from school. You remember him? He was very good at maths. Got medals, exhibitions, scholarships etc. McHenry of our class has not turned up since school opened last Wednesday. Miss Ryan the French professor and her assistant [Mr] Brien are arrested. The English are howling about German outrages in Belgium, but what they themselves did in Dublin puts everyting into the shade. I suppose you saw the account of the young volunteer who would not inform, in [John] Dillon's speech. There were seventeen men murdered by them in [North] King Street. One boy in Great Georges Street got seven bullets in him while in bed ([he was] fifteen years of age). They fired indiscriminately in all directions. Fortunately they were wretched shots. Most of them were about a month, I think, in the army. Fr Egan said they were standing shaking [?] the moment they saw a sign of life. An officer told him that he was in the battle of Ypres, but [that] it was nothing to Dublin. The soldiers entered Sir Patrick Dun's Hospital to throw grenades from it. They fired on the Royal Engineers at Lansdowne Road and these replied with grenades, inflicting some damage and giving them a very good [chance] of going [down]. The Volunteers had a magnificent body of sharpshooters. One man disabled three machine guns from the Post Office by [hitting] them in one vulnerable spot. A man in Talbot Street shot seventeen soldiers – one near Church Street killed five. Some firing is still going on – three officers being killed on Friday last. It is said there is a mutiny of the Irish soldiers in the Curragh. Duckie has a copy of the charge against Jack. It is perfectly general – something about waging war against the King, i.e., His Brittanic Majesty, and being prejudicial to the Defence of the Realm with the intent of helping the enemy. She says they were tried in batches, the evidence being taken against each separately. In the fight the losses of the Irish were very small. One man [was] killed at the Four Courts, one or two in the Mendicity [Institution], none at Jacob's, [and] a few at Boland's, but they lost sixty-eight at Stephen's Green and a large number at the Post Office. You cannot believe a word the papers say! The English lost 137 killed! Why thirty-four bodies were taken out of Cole's Lane! They were slain in hundreds at the Four Courts and at Beggars Bush. They charged nine times into the square of the Four Courts, only to be mowed down. One regiment – the Irish Rifles – was 109 short in its roll call after fighting at Jacobs. A regiment marched from the Curragh and lay down to rest at Dolphin's Barn. They were set on by the

Irish with machine guns and massacred. A [dozen] volunteers on Blacquiere Bridge kept a regiment at bay for two days. An account is given in the *Daily Mail* of the gallant way the lancers charged in O'Connell Street and cleared it of the rebels. The truth as by an eyewitness is that [they] trotted gaily along, their lances in the air. Ten Volunteers came out, knelt and fired emptying a few saddles and the lancers fled in confusion. Another account says that one of them spoke to the Captain, 'come on, they have only blank cartridges.' 'Blank or not', said he and he turned [?] and at the same moment the man who had spoken fell dead. After the charge at [St] Stephens Green they left Harcourt Street strewn with their dead. I have heard many other things which I dare not write. The brother of one of our lay brothers had something of an experience. He is a soldier and was arrested by the volunteers on Easter Monday. He was lodged in a cellar in Queen Street. The house went on fire and the Volunteers had to evacuate it. He escaped and wandered down to Abbey Street without being [retaken]. Here he was called into another cellar by some other soldiers. He house was burned [over] them and they were the whole week without food. At last he heard a great noise in the street and he came out. The Lancers were making their way back, and he [ran] with them and got to the English lines.

Fr [F?] [gave] the number of English killed as something over 2,000. The Volunteers could [have held] out much longer but for Pearse's [surrender] notice. By the way, he said he could not believe a word of the papers after seeing big lies in them which he knew personally to be such.

I went over to the Mendicity again today (Tuesday) and got into it. The people were put out on Easter Monday by the Volunteers. The soldiers they shot down were diagonally across the river on the other side of [it], and so were at a considerable distance. They must have been good marksmen to single out the officers and kill them at such a distance; much better then the soldiers. Fr Egan said these, from a distance of fifty yards at Boland's, covered the walls with pieces of lead yet hardly got a few into the windows. Fr F saw a number lined up in Dorset Street firing at a window on the opposite side. The shots went all round the windows without a single one getting in. It is, of course, quite evident that Jack's pistols could not have carried across the river. The soldiers then surrounded the institute, cutting off the means of retreat. The man who showed me round told me he walked up and down several times looking at the place and he saw not a single Volunteer at the windows. The soldiers here seem to have been good shots, for I saw few traces on the outside but the inside was full of holes. The direction of the holes showed that shots had come from above and below them on the quays, and I think some even from the other side of the river possibly from the roofs of the house for a few of the holes were lowdown lower even than the window sills. There were two or three holes right through the floor. This was where one of the Volunteers was badly wounded. The man said the place was full of blood here. These were, of course, the work of the grenades. He said [that] to throw these. the soldiers came round quite close under cover of some low walls. When they succeeded in getting them in, the Volunteers held out no time. One of the Volunteers, he said, took a gold pin away. This was found on him at Arbour Hill. I hope that is not true. Some of the soldiers [quietly removed] about £9 or £10 of his. He said including broken furniture, etc, there was about £60 [of] damage done.

The other night Jack told me to tell mother, indeed I think he told her himself afterwards, that if anyone asked for any of his books she was to give them, so I was thinking of getting them here for the novitiate. Four of us always or nearly always talk Irish wherever two of us are together, so there is practically always one pair or perhaps more talking Irish at recreations. We had teaching in Irish on St Patrick's night in the refectory. The week of the Rising (which I suppose you heard of as a Larkinite riot as it was published in Cork at least. By the way did you see the letter the coadjutor bishop of Cork wrote to the papers? You should see it as a sample of British treachery) there was the largest naval engagement of the war. It is impossible to get the true news now, of course, since the Volunteers no longer exist, but it is said that twelve English battleships went down. They have acknowledged the loss of one and this is the only reference to it in the papers, so it does not look at though England has anything to [hug] herself about. I heard today that Gahan was in Jacob's and Kelly in the Post Office where he was wounded the first day, and [from] where he was brought to Jervis Street and thence to England. I had written you a long letter like this on Easter Sunday, but it was impossible to post it and as events turned out I destroyed it. I hope to hear from you in the day or two. Fr Michael would not show me the letter you wrote him, but be sure you could not say anything too good about him. He was wonderfully kind during the last few [weeks]. You would really have thought it was his own brother. I hope you will excuse the disjointed style of this letter. I put everything down as it came to my head. A word about theologians. You may meet some of them condemning the Rising as unjustifiable – we have some here. Don't believe them – it is only their own private opinion and Fr F is against them there. Of course everybody says that it was perfectly lawful for the individuals. The volunteers tried to blow up the Magazine Hill but it was absolutely empty.

Goodbye. Your affectionate brother, Bro. John Heuston.

PS: the man at the Mendicity told me no Volunteers were killed there. Two or three were wounded. Bro. John.

APPENDIX 2:

Allen Library, ROI/134. This anonymous broadside is of unknown provenance, but is likely to have been printed in the years immediately after 1916. Readers can judge for themselves what relationship it bears to the reality of Heuston's life. It is reproduced here by permission of the Allen Library.

To Seán Heuston.

Oh! Brave and young Seán Heuston, who died for truth and right
And gave your life to free our land from Britain's greed and might;
Who strove to raise our flag on high by men erect and free,
And keep it above the pirate red and free from slavery.

You rose with men to right a wrong witheld our land for years
And end all shame and slavery accursed in blood and tears,
And when Erin called you in her need you went and proudly gave
The sunshine of your happiness for the silence of the grave.

You were proud and brave and daring, when in war's greatest need,
With the free-born Oglaig na h-Eireann [sic] you sowed freedom's seed,
And with the young Fianna who work for all that's grand,
You taught and trained unceasingly to guard our native land.

Your life you pledged to the Irish land, that once had been serene,
And England's flag to lower again beneath our Irish green;

To overthrow the Saxon power of evil, crime and shame,
Its strength to stifle in bloody fray by men of soldier's fame.

All coward slaveling you despised as you spurned the cruel guilt
Of begging or of crawling to the tyrant law and filth,
Its spies it used to track you down in night as well as day,
But their vigilance you baffled oft in your own drear way.

But when at last they had you in their vile and evil hands
They perjured and they murdered you by cold blooded bands
Because you fought for Ireland's rights our country's liberty,
And commanded men in Dublin town who fought to be free.

They shattered you whose manly form in life they could not bend,
These Saxon hordes of guilt and crime, your life they craved to end
And while your blood was warm ere your spirit to Heaven had
flown
They flung you in a quick-lime grave nameless and unknown.

Such was the death they gave to you who loved this land so well
Who worked and fought unflinchingly the foreign power to quel
Such is the fate of freedom's sons who work to free their land
From oppression and slavery, wrought by a murderous hand.

We'll bear it all in freedom's name as men have borne before,
The dungeon and the prison cell, the scaffold grim and sore,
But while we live upon this land on hill or crag or plain
We swear revenge for him and all who were so basely slain.

We'll ring it to the heavens above we'll shout it high and low,
We'll send it o'er the ocean waves where brave hearts rise and grow,
To lands remote and distant where freemen proudly dwell,
We must revenge Seán Heuston's death, by rifle shot and shell.

Farewell to him so true and brave, may he in peace now rest,
With they who have borne the cross of pain with manly breast
Have faced the rifle muzzle, suffered cell or scaffold high,
And for freedom and for justice died without fear or faltering sigh.

BIBLIOGRAPHY

MANUSCRIPTS:

Allen Library, Dublin:
Seán Heuston papers.
ROI/134: 'To Seán Heuston.'
MS 201/file b: Diary of Madeleine ffrench-Mullen.

General Registry Office, Dublin:
Indexes to civil births, deaths and marriages.

Kilmainham Gaol Museum, Dublin:
Seán Heuston papers

Military Archives, Cathal Brugha Barracks, Dublin:
Bureau of Military History: witness statements and contemporary documents
(witness statements are online at http://www.bureauofmilitaryhistory.ie/).

National Archives of Ireland:
1901 and 1911 census returns
(online at http://www.census.nationalarchives.ie/).

National Archives of the United Kingdom:
War Office papers: WO 71/351.

National Library of Ireland:
Liam Mellows, *The Irish Boy Scouts* (NLI 1A 2302).
MS 10,076: 'Two documents on the career of Seán Heuston in the G.S. &
W.R.'.
MS 15,047: 'Two letters of Seán Heuston'.
MS 36,147: Patrick J. Stephenson, 'Heuston's Fort: the Mendicity Institute

Easter Week 1916'.

Irish Railway Record Society Archives

Great Southern and Western Railway collection.

NEWSPAPERS AND PERIODICALS

Capuchin Annual

Camillian Post

The Catholic Bulletin and Book Review

Irish Freedom

Gaelic American

Fianna

Wolfe Tone Annual

Worker's Republic

BOOKS AND ARTICLES:

Barton, Brian, *The secret court martial records of the Easter rising* (Stroud, 2010).

Brady, Joseph and Simms, Anngret (eds), Dublin through Space and Time, *c.900- c.1900 (Dublin, 2001).*

Campbell, Fergus *The Irish Establishment, 1879-1914* (Oxford, 2009).

Casey, Christine, *Dublin: The City within the Grand and Royal Canals and the Circular Road with the Phoenix Park (New Haven, 2005).*

Coldrey, Barry, *Faith and Fatherland: the Christian Brothers and the development of Irish nationalism, 1838-1921 (Dublin, 1987).*

Corlett, Christiaan, *Darkest Dublin: the story of the Church Street disaster and a pictorial account of the slums of Dublin in 1913 (Dublin, 2008).*

Daly, Mary 'Social Structure of the Dublin working class, 1871-1911', *Irish Historical Studies 23 (1982), pp 121-33.*

Daly, Mary E., *Dublin, the Deposed Capital: A Social and Economic History, 1860-1900 (Cork, 1984).*

Dickson, David, 'Death of a capital? Dublin and the consequences of Union', *in Peter Clarke and Raymond Gillespie (eds), Two Capitals: London and Dublin, 1500-1840 (Oxford, 2001), pp 111-31.*

Dictionary of Irish Biography (9 vols, Cambridge, 2009).

Dublin's fighting story, 1916-21; told by the men who made it (Cork, 2009).

Fianna Handbook (Dublin, 1914?: NLI Ir 367 f. 16).

Fitzpatrick, David, 'Militarism in Ireland, 1900–1922', in Thomas Bartlett and

   Keith Jeffrey (eds), A military history of Ireland (Cambridge, 1996), pp 379-406.

Foy, Michael T., and Brian Barton, *The Easter Rising* (2nd ed., Stroud, 2011).

Griffith, Kenneth, and O'Grady, Timothy, *Curious journey: an oral history of Ire

   land's unfinished revolution (London, 1982).*

Hay, Marnie, 'This treasured island: Irish nationalist propaganda aimed at

   children and youth, 1919-16', in Mary Shine Thompson & Celia Keenan (eds),

   Treasure islands: studies in children's literature (Dublin, 2006), pp 33-42.

Hay, Marnie, 'The foundation and development of Na Fianna Éireann, 1909-

   16', Irish Historical Studies 36 (May 2008), pp 53-71.

Heuston, John M. [Michael], *Headquarters battalion, Easter week 1916* (Carlow,

   1966?).

Horne, John, 'Masculinity in politics and war in the age of nation-states and

   world wars, 1850-1950', in Stefan Dudiek, Karen Hagenamm, and John Tosh

   (eds), Masculinities in politics and war: gendering modern history (Manchester, 2004),

   pp 22-40.

Irish History Reader; by the Christian Brothers (Dublin, 1905).

Jeffrey, Keith, *Ireland and the Great War* (Cambridge, 2000).

Joyce, James, *Dubliners* (Dublin: O'Brien Press, 2012).

Lee, Joseph, 'The golden age of Irish railways', in Kevin B. Nowlam (ed), *Travel

   and transport in Ireland (Dublin, 1973).*

Limerick's Fighting Story, 1916-21: Told by the men who made it (Cork, 2009).

McGarry, Fearghal, *The Rising: Ireland: Easter 1916* (Oxford, 2010).

McGarry, Fearghal, *Rebels: Voices from the Easter Rising* (London, 2011).

Griffith, Kenneth, and Timothy O'Grady, *Curious journey: an oral history of Ire

   land's unfinished revolution (London, 1982).*

Mac Lochlainn, Piaras F., *Last Words: Letters and statements of the leaders executed

   after the rising at Easter 1916 (Dublin, 1990).*

Milne, Kenneth, *The Dublin Liberties, 1600-1850* (Dublin, 2009).

Murray, K.A., and D.B. McNeill, *The GSWR Railway* (Dublin, 1976).

Kevin B. Nowlam, 'The transport revolution: the coming of the railways', in

   idem (ed), Travel and transport in Ireland (Dublin, 1973).

O'Brien, J.V., *'Dear, dirty Dublin': a city in distress, 1899-1916* (Berkeley, CA, & London, 1982).

O'Callaghan, John, *Revolutionary Limerick: the republican campaign for independence in Limerick, 1913-1921 (Dublin, 2010)*.

Ó Colmáin, Risteárd, 'Colmán Ó Sórd Colmcille', *ESB Journal: Easter Rising Commemorative Edition,, vol. 8.9 (April 1966), pp 35-38*.

O Droighneáin, Muiris, (ed), *An Sloinnteoir Gaeilge agus an tAinmneoir* (Belfast 1966; 2nd ed, Micheal Ailf O Murchu (ed), Dublin, 1999)*.

Ó Ruairc, Pádraig Óg, *Revolution: A photographic history of revolutionary Ireland, 1913-1923 (Cork, 2011)*.

Pearse, Pádraig, *Political writings and speeches* (Dublin, 1952).

Rigney, Peter, 'Easter Week 1916 and the Great Southern & Western Railway', *Journal of the Irish Railway Record Society, 22: 160 (2006), pp 458-61*.

Thom's Directory.

Townsend, Charles, *Easter 1916: the Irish rebellion* (London, 2006).

Whelan, Kevin, 'The memories of 'The Dead'', *Yale Journal of Criticism*, 15.1 *(Spring 2002), pp 59-97*.

Woods, Audrey, *Dublin Outsiders: A history of the Mendicity Institution, 1818-1998 (Dublin, 1999)*.

Yeates, Padraig, *A city in wartime: Dublin 1914-18* (Dublin, 2011).

NOTES

1. Piaras F. Mac Lochlainn, *Last Words: Letters and statements of the leaders executed after the rising at Easter 1916* (Dublin, 1990), p. 110. The original is retained in Kilmainham Gaol Museum: 17 LR IC45 12.

2. Mac Lochlainn, *Last Words,* p. 110.

3. Unless otherwise indicated, the following details of the visit, and of the the the conversation that ensued, are taken from Michael Heuston's own account: see Bureau of Military History (BMH), Contemporary Documents (CD) 309/1, ff 1-4.

4. Mac Lochlainn, *Last Words,* p. 113.

5. Mac Lochlainn, *Last Words*, pp 108–09.

6. BMH CD 309/1, ff 14-15.

7. Unless otherwise indicated, all information on the family in this chapter is derived from the relevant General Registration Office (GRO) records of civil births and marriages.

8. Kilmainham, Heuston MS 07 LG IC45 15; 09 LG IC45 16. The indexes to civil registration record only one Maria McDonald born in the registration district of Dublin North in 1867; the actual birth certificate lists the family surname as 'McDonnell'. Certain details on the 1867 civil birth record of Maria McDonnell correspond with the 1888 marriage record of John Heuston and Maria McDonald. The father of the bride in 1888 was recorded as John McDonald, a porter; the same name and occupation recorded on the 1867 birth certificate.

9. Mary Daly, 'Social Structure of the Dublin working class, 1871-1911', *Irish Historical Studies* 23 (1982), pp 125-26.

10. This discussion is based on Joseph Brady and Anngret Simms (eds), *Dublin through Space and Time, c. 900-c. 1900* (Dublin, 2001); Christine Casey, *Dublin: The City within the Grand and Royal Canals and the Circular Road with the Phoenix Park* (New Haven, 2005); Mary E. Daly, *Dublin, the Deposed Capital: A Social and Economic History, 1860-1900* (Cork, 1984); and David Dickson, 'Death of a capital? Dublin and the consequences of Union', in Peter Clarke and Raymond

Gillespie (eds), *Two Capitals: London and Dublin, 1500-1840* (Oxford, 2001) pp 111-31.

11. J.V. O'Brien, *'Dear, dirty Dublin': a city in distress, 1899-1916* (Berkeley, CA, & London, 1982), pp 23, 132-33.

12. All information on the family in this section is derived from civil birth records, and the relevant census returns for 1901, available online at http://www.census.nationalarchives.ie/).

13. O'Brien, *'Dear dirty Dublin'*, p. 112.

14. This is the subject of Christian Corlett, *Darkest Dublin: the story of the Church Street disaster and a pictorial account of the slums of Dublin in 1913* (Dublin, 2008).

15. Handwritten notes by P.J. Stephenson: Jim Stephenson, private collection.

16. Barry Coldrey, *Faith and Fatherland: the Christian Brothers and the development of Irish nationalism, 1838-1921* (Dublin, 1987), pp 113-39, 159-64.

17. *Irish History Reader,* by the Christian Brothers (Dublin, 1905), pp 339-40.

18. 'Heuston's heroic mother', *Gaelic American,* 11 Nov. 1916.

19. Handwritten notes by P.J. Stephenson: Jim Stephenson, private collection.

20. National Library of Ireland (NLI) MS 10,076; 1911 census returns.

21. *Thom's Directory,* 1906; 1908.

22. Allen Library, Heuston collection: GSWR application form completed by John J. Heuston, 21 June 1907. A photostat is retained in the National Library: NLI MS 10,076.

23. Fergus Campbell, *The Irish Establishment, 1879-1914* (Oxford, 2009), p. 196.

24. Kevin B. Nowlam, 'The transport revolution: the coming of the railways', in idem (ed), *Travel and transport in Ireland* (Dublin, 1973), p. 109.

25. Nowlam, 'The transport revolution'; Joseph Lee, 'The golden age of Irish railways' in Nowlam (ed), *Travel and transport in Ireland*, pp 110-19. See also K.A. Murray & D.B. McNeill, *The GSW Railway* (Dublin, 1976).

26. Fergus Campbell, *Irish Establishment*, p. 191; p. 191 n.1.

27. Ibid., p. 241; p. 241 n.181.

28. Irish Railway Records Society Archives (IRRSA): GSWR Secretary's Office File 365. The phrase is taken from Fearghal McGarry, *The Rising: Ireland: Easter 1916* (Oxford, 2010).

29. Lee, 'The golden age of Irish railways'.

30. Allen Library, Heuston papers: medical form and 'Declaration of fidelity and

secrecy', 1 Aug 1907.

31. Allen Library, Heuston papers: 'Special report to be made respecting clerks on probation: John Joseph Heuston', 12 Sept 1908. A photostat copy is retained as NLI MS 10,076.

32. Allen Library, Heuston papers: 'Examination papers for goods departments clerks' [Mr J. Heuston, Limerick], 29 Sept. 1908.

33. All information on the Heuston family in this section is derived from the relevant 1911 census returns for Dublin and Limerick.

34. Mac Lochlainn, *Last Words*, p. 115.

35. Unless otherwise indicated, all details on Na Fianna, including the spelling of the relevant terms in Irish, are drawn from Marnie Hay, 'The foundation and development of Na Fianna Éireann, 1909-16', *Irish Historical Studies* (May 2008), pp 53-71; Fearghal McGarry, *Rebels: Voices from the Easter Rising* (London, 2011), pp 47-61.

36. Pádraig Pearse, *Political writings and speeches* (Dublin, 1952), pp 114–116.

37. McGarry, *Rebels*, p. 48.

38. John Horne, 'Masculinity in politics and war in the age of nation-states and world wars, 1850-1950', in Stefan Dudiek, Karen Hagenamm, and John Tosh (eds), *Masculinities in politics and war: gendering modern history* (Manchester, 2004), pp 22-40.

39. David Fitzpatrick, 'Militarism in Ireland, 1900-1922', in Thomas Bartlett and Keith Jeffrey (eds), *A military history of Ireland* (Cambridge, 1996), pp 379-406.

40. BMH WS 755 (Seán Prendergast), section 1, p. 90.

41. *Fianna Handbook* (Dublin, 1914: NLI Ir 367 f. 16): p. 6.

42. Ibid., p. 7.

43. Ibid., p. 8.

44. Ibid., p. 13.

45. Ibid., pp 14-15.

46. Ibid., pp 75-86.

47. Ibid., pp 151-65.

48. Ibid., p. 167.

49. *Irish Freedom*, June 1912.

50. Ibid., Feb. 1913.

51. BMH Witness Statement (WS) 1420 (Patrick Whelan), p. 2.

52. Allen Library, Heuston papers: Answer papers for GWSR clerkship exam, c.1907, no. 496.

53. *Irish Freedom*, Sept. 1911; Aug. 1912.

54. *Limerick's Fighting Story, 1916-21: Told by the men who made it* (Cork, 2009), p. 75.

55. Ibid., pp. 75-76.

56. John O'Callaghan, *Revolutionary Limerick: the republican campaign for independence in Limerick, 1913-1921* (Dublin, 2010), p. 31.

57. Hay, 'Foundation and development of Na Fianna Éireann', p. 59.

58. BMH WS 1420 (Patrick Whelan), p. 2.

59. *Irish Freedom,* Jan. 1913.

60. *Irish Freedom*, Jan. 1913.

61. BMH WS 1420 (Patrick Whelan), pp 2-3.

62. *Irish Freedom*, June 1913.

63. BMH WS 1420 (Patrick Whelan), p. 3.

64. *Irish Freedom*, Aug.1913.

65. *Irish Freedom,* Jan. 1914. 'Mac Aodha' translates literally as 'McHugh'. Heuston is a distinctive name but is not of Irish origin: *An Sloinnteoir Gaeilge agus an tAinmneoir,* edited by Muiris O Droighneáin (Belfast: Irish News, 1966) suggests Mac Giolla tSeachlainn for Heuston: p. 36. The updated and expanded version by Micheal Ailf O Murchu (Dublin, 1999) offers Mac Aodha for Heuson: p. 49. The 1999 volume does not contain an equivalent for Heuston and the 1996 edition does not offer an equivalent for Heuson. My thanks to Brian O Conchubair for clarification on this point.

66. *Fianna Handbook* (NLI Ir 367 f. 16): pp 17-23.

67. Liam Mellows, 'The Irish Boy Scouts' (NLI 1A 2302), p. 9. This text is based on articles written by Mellows for the *Gaelic American* in 1917.

68. IRRSA, GSWR Traffic Staff Register No. 14, p. 5.

69. BMH WS 150 (Gregory Murphy), pp 1-2; BMH WS 170 (Peter Paul Galligan), pp 1-2; BMH WS 818 (Jack Stafford), p. 1.

70. BMH WS 1377 (Aodh MacNeill), p. 8; BMH WS 280 (Robert Holland), p. 3.

71. *Irish Freedom*, Feb. 1914.

72. BMH WS 755 (Seán Prendergast), section 1, p. 64; BMH WS 328 (Gearoid Ua h-Uallachain [sic]), p. 34.

73. BMH WS 755 (Seán Prendergast), section 1, p. 65.

74. Ibid., p. 66

75. Ibid., pp 68–69.

76. BMH WS 328 (Gearoid Ua h-Uallachain [sic]), pp 39–40; BMH WS 755 (Seán Prendergast), section 1, p. 69.

77. BMH WS 1043 (Joseph V. Lawless), p. 4.

78. Ibid., p. 5; BMH WS 328 (Gearoid Ua h-Uallachain [sic]), p. 40.

79. BMH WS 755 (Seán Prendergast), section 1, p. 70.

80. Ibid., p. 72; BMH WS 328 (Gearoid Ua h-Uallachain [sic]), p. 39.

81. BMH WS 328 (Gearoid Ua h-Uallachain [sic]), p. 41.

82. BMH WS 755 (Seán Prendergast), section 1, p. 76.

83. Ibid., p. 79.

84. Ibid., p. 82.

85. *Dublin's fighting story, 1916-21; told by the men who made it* (Cork, 2009), p. 210.

86. BMH WS 755 (Seán Prendergast), section 1, pp 84–86.

87. BMH WS 1670 (Seamus Kavanagh), p. 17.

88. BMH WS 755 (Seán Prendergast), section 1, pp 66, 80.

89. BMH WS 411 (Eamon Morkan), p. 2.

90. BMH WS 282 (Charles J. O'Grady), p. 2.

91. Padraig Yeates, *A city in wartime: Dublin 1914-18* (Dublin, 2011), pp 44–45.

92. For wartime Dublin prior to the Easter Rising see ibid., pp 1–89.

93. Marnie Hay, 'This treasured island: Irish nationalist propaganda aimed at children and youth, 1919-16', in Mary Shine Thompson and Celia Keenan (eds), *Treasure islands: studies in children's literature* (Dublin, 2006), pp 33–42.

94. Fianna, Aug. 1915.

95. BMH WS 191 (Joseph Reynolds), p. 3.

96. BMH WS 201 (Nicholas Laffan), p. 2.

97. NLI MS 36,147: Patrick J. Stephenson, 'Heuston's Fort: the Mendicity Institute Easter Week 1916' [Dated 1966]. According to the foreword, signed by his sons, the memoir was 'written by the late P.J. Stephenson some few years after the event'; it was now being made 'available for private circulation to his family

and friends during this year of celebration of the fiftieth anniversary of Easter Week': vii.

98. Stephenson, 'Heuston's Fort', pp 1-2.

99. Ibid., p. 2.

100. Ibid., p. 2.

101. Ibid., p. 3.

102. BMH WS 1219 (Seán O'Neill), p. 20.

103. BMH WS 328 (Gearoid Ua h-Uallachain [sic]), p. 35.

104. BMH WS 755 (Seán Prendergast), section 1, pp 90-91.

105. Ibid., pp 103-04.

106. BMH WS 781 (Patrick J. Kelly), p. 6.

107. BMH WS 192 (Fionan Lynch), p. 7.

108. Stephenson, 'Heuston's Fort', p. 4.

109. BMH WS 1377 (Aodh MacNeill), p. 12.

110. Stephenson, 'Heuston's Fort', p. 5.

111. John M. [Michael] Heuston, O.P, Headquarters battalion, Easter week 1916 (Carlow, 1966?), p. 16.

112. Stephenson, 'Heuston's Fort', p. 3.

113. Ibid., p. 3.

114. Ibid., p. 3.

115. Ibid., p. 4.

116. BMH CD 309/1 f. 5.

117. Stephenson, 'Heuston's Fort', p. 6.

118. BMH CD 309/1, f. 15.

119. BMH WS 276 (Charles S. McQuaile), p. 2.

120. Charles Townsend, *Easter 1916: the Irish rebellion* (London, 2006), pp 131-33.

121. Townsend, *Easter 1916*, pp 143-51; McGarry, *The Rising*, pp 1-2.

122. BMH WS 276 (Charles S. McQuaile), pp 2-3.

123. BMH CD 309/1, ff 6, 15-16.

124. BMH WS 201 (Nicholas Laffan), p. 3.

125. Stephenson, 'Heuston's Fort', p. 6; Jim Stephenson, private collection.

126. Stephenson, 'Heuston's Fort', pp 6-7.

127. Stephenson, 'Heuston's Fort', p. 7.

128. James J. Brennan, 'The Mendicity Institution Area', *Capuchin Annual* (1966), p. 190.

129. BMH WS 284 (Michael Staines), p. 8.

130. Ibid., p. 9.

131. BMH WS 943 (Michael Staines), p. 1.

132. Stephenson, 'Heuston's Fort', pp 7-8.

133. BMH WS 923 (Ignatius Callendar), p. 3.

134. BMH WS 284 (Michael Staines), p. 9.

135. BMH WS 943 (Michael Staines), p. 1; BMH WS 923 (Ignatius Callendar), p. 4.

136. Stephenson, 'Heuston's Fort', p. 8.

137. BMH CD 309/1, ff 16-24.

138. Stephenson, 'Heuston's Fort', p. 9.

139. BMH CD 309/1, f. 17.

140. Stephenson, 'Heuston's Fort', p. 11.

141. Ibid., p. 12.

142. Ibid., p. 12.

143. BMH WS 276 (Charles S. McQuaile), p. 3.

144. Stephenson, 'Heuston's Fort', p. 12.

145. Stephenson, 'Heuston's Fort', p. 13.

146. Stephenson, 'Heuston's Fort', p. 13.

147. BMH WS 923 (Ignatius Callendar), p. 5.

148. Stephenson, 'Heuston's Fort', p. 13.

149. Ibid., p. 14.

150. James Joyce, *Dubliners* (Dublin: O'Brien Press, 2012), p. 198. All quotations are from this edition.

151. For the Mendicity Institution see Audrey Woods, *Dublin Outsiders: A history of the Mendicity Institution,* 1818-1998 (Dublin, 1999).

152. Kenneth Milne, *The Dublin Liberties, 1600-1850* (Dublin, 2009), pp 14-15. For Dublin's decline after 1800 see Dickson, 'Death of a capital?'.

153. Kevin Whelan, 'The memories of 'The Dead'', *Yale Journal of Criticism*, 15.1 (Spring 2002), pp 59-97.

154. Joyce, *Dubliners,* pp 198-99.

155. Ibid., p. 233.

156. Ibid., pp 221.

157. Woods, *Dublin Outsiders*, p. 174.

158. Joyce, *Dubliners*, p. 229.

159. 'Setanta' [James Connolly], 'The Mendicity and its guests', *Worker's Republic*, 27 Aug. 1898.

160 .Woods, *Dublin Outsiders*, p. 172.

161. BMH WS 563 (Michael Cremen), p. 3.

162. BMH WS 328 (Gearoid Ua h-Uallachain [sic]), pp 52-53. Dick Balfe made a similar claim, but went so far as to claim that he was in fact the person detailed to command the post at the Mendicity Institute, and that Heuston had simply tagged along: a claim that is flatly contradicted by the available evidence: BMH 251 (Richard Balfe), p. 5.

163. BMH CD 309/1, f. 18.

164. BMH CD 309/2.

165. BMH WS 242 (Liam Tannam), p. 8.

166. Daly, Deposed Capital, pp 23-30; Brady and Simms, *Dublin through space and time,* pp 303-08.

167. Michael T. Foy and Brian Barton, *The Easter Rising* (2nd ed., Stroud, 2011), p. 148.

168. Peter Rigney, 'Easter Week 1916 and the Great Southern & Western Railway', *Journal of the Irish Railway Record Society,* 22: 160 (2006), pp 458-61.

169. Stephenson, 'Heuston's Fort', p. 14.

170. Ibid., p. 14.

171. Woods, *Dublin Outsiders*, p. 173.

172. BMH 251 (Dick Balfe), p. 5.

173. Brennan, 'The Mendicity Institution Area', p. 190.

174. Stephenson, 'Heuston's Fort', p. 15.

175. Ibid., p. 16.

176. BMH CD 309/1 f.18.

177. Stephenson, 'Heuston's Fort', p. 16.

178. Ibid., 16-17.

179. BMH WS 290 (Seán McLoughlin), p. 8.

180. Seán McLoughlin, 'Memories of the Easter Rising, 1916', *Camillian Post*, vol. 13 no 1 (Spring 1948), p. 6.

181. BMH CD 309/1, f.19.

182. Stephenson, 'Heuston's Fort', p. 17.

183. BMH WS 251 (Dick Balfe), p. 5.

184. My thanks to Shane MacThomais for these details.

185. Brennan, 'The Mendicity Institution Area', p. 190.

186. BMH CD 309/1,

187. Stephenson, 'Heuston's Fort', p. 17.

188. BMH CD 309/1, p.19

189. Stephenson, 'Heuston's Fort', p. 18.

190. Ibid., p. 18.

191. Ibid., p. 18.

192. BMH WS 251 (Dick Balfe), p. 5.

193. BMH WS 290 (Seán McLoughlin), p. 8.

194. Stephenson, 'Heuston's Fort', p. 19.

195. McLoughlin, 'Memories of the Easter Rising, 1916', p. 6.

196. BMH WS 290 (Seán McLoughlin), p. 9–10; BMH CD 309/1, f. 20.

197. Ibid., ff 20–21.

198. BMH WS 290 (Seán McLoughlin), p. 10.

199. BMH WS 735 (Charles J. MacAuley), p. 4.

200. BMH WS 194 (Domnhall Ó Buachalla), p. 2.

201. BMH WS 251 (Dick Balfe), p. 6.

202. Brennan, 'The Mendicity Institution Area', p. 190.

203. BMH CD 309/1, f. 21.

204. Stephenson, 'Heuston's Fort', p. 19.

205. See appendix 1.

206. Stephenson, 'Heuston's Fort', p. 19.

207. Ibid., p. 20.

208. Ibid., p. 21.

209. McLoughlin, 'Memories of the Easter Rising, 1916', p. 7.

210. BM WS 251 (Dick Balfe), p. 6.

211. Stephenson, 'Heuston's Fort', p. 22.

212. BMH CD 309/1, f. 21.

213. National Archives of the United Kingdom (NAUK), WO 71/351.

214. BMH WS 290 (Seán McLoughlin), p. 11.

215. BMH WS 251 (Dick Balfe), p. 6.

216. Stephenson, 'Heuston's Fort', p. 24.

217. Stephenson, 'Heuston's Fort', p. 31.

218. McLoughlin, 'Memories of the Easter Rising, 1916', p. 8.

219. Stephenson, 'Heuston's Fort', p. 25.

220. Ibid, p. 25.

221. BMH WS 251 (Dick Balfe), pp 6-7.

222. Brennan, 'The Mendicity Institution Area', p. 191.

223. BMH CD 309/1, f. 21.

224. BMH WS 148 (James Crenigan), p. 3.

225. Stephenson, 'Heuston's Fort', p. 26.

226. McLoughlin, 'Memories of the Easter Rising, 1916', p. 8; BMH WS 290 (Seán McLoughlin), p. 12.

227. BMH CD 309/1, ff 21-22.

228. Barton & Foy, Easter Rising, p. 159.

229. BMH WS 1399 (Thomas Peppard), p. 4.

230. Stephenson, 'Heuston's Fort', pp 24-25.

231. Ibid., p. 26.

232. Risteárd Ó Colmáin, 'Colmán Ó Sórd Colmcille', *ESB Journal: Easter Rising Commemorative Edition*, vol. 8.9 (April 1966), p. 36.

233. BMH WS 148 (James Crenigan), pp 3-4.

234. Stephenson, 'Heuston's Fort', p. 26.

235. According to Michael Heuston, 'during the night a detachment of eighty or a hundred soldier passed along. The Volunteers let them come right under the windows and then opened on them. They could not escape and the Volunteers could not miss the mass just in front of them. Scarce one escaped unwounded. This showed where the Volunteers were. I do not know whether this occurred on Monday or Tuesday night': BMH CD 309/1, f. 21.

236. Stephenson, 'Heuston's Fort', p. 27-29.

237. Ó Colmáin, 'Colmán Ó Sórd Colmcille', p. 37.

238. Brennan, 'The Mendicity Institution Area', p. 191.

239. BMH WS 1399 (Thomas Peppard), p. 5.

240. BMH CD 309/1, ff 22-23.

241. Brennan, 'The Mendicity Institution Area', p. 191.

242. BMH CD 309/1, ff. 23.

243. Ibid., ff 23-24.

244. Brennan, 'The Mendicity Institution Area', p. 191.

245. BMH CD 309/1, f. 24.

246. Brennan, 'The Mendicity Institution Area', p. 191.

247. BMH WS 251 (Dick Balfe), p. 7.

248. BMH WS 259 (Dr. B. Thornton), p. 4.

249. BMH WS 842 (Seán Kennedy), p. 15.

250. McLoughlin, 'Memories of the Easter Rising, 1916', p. 8; BMH WS 290 (Seán McLoughlin), pp 13-14.

251. Stephenson, 'Heuston's Fort', p. 29.

252. Stephenson, 'Heuston's Fort', pp 29-31; McLoughlin, 'Memories of the Easter Rising, 1916' p. 8

253. Stephenson, 'Heuston's Fort', p. 31.

254. BMH WS 923 (Ignatius Callender), pp 13, 21.

255. BMH CD 309/4.

256. BMH CD 309/1, f. 25.

257. All details from NAUK WO 71/351; Brian Barton, The secret court martial records of the Easter rising (Stroud, 2010), pp 259-61.

258. Barton, Secret court martial records, pp 41, 43.

259. NLI MS 15,047.

260. Barton, Secret court martial records, p. 251.

261. BMH WS 805 (Annie O'Brien and Lily Curran), pp 12-13.

262. See BMH CD 309/1, *passim*. Unless otherwise indicated, all details and quotations in this chapter have been taken from this account.

263. Mac Lochlainn, Last Words, pp 110-11.

264. Keith Jeffrey, *Ireland and the Great War* (Cambridge, 2000), p. 53.

265. Mac Lochlainn, Last Words, pp 113-14.

266. Ibid., p. 112.

267. Ibid., p. 112.

268. Mac Lochlainn, Last Words, p. 114.

269. Kilmainham Gaol Museum, Heuston papers: 17 LR IC45 03.

270. 'How Seán Heuston died: From a letter by the late Father Albert, O.M. Cap', *Capuchin Annual: 1935* (Dublin, 1935), pp 162-64; Mac Lochlainn, Last

Words, pp 114–16.

271. Allen Library, MS 201/file b.

272. Kenneth Griffith and Timothy O'Grady, *Curious journey: an oral history of Ireland's unfinished revolution* (London, 1982), p. 86.

273. BMH CD 309/1, f. 6.

274. 'Heuston's heroic mother', *Gaelic American,* 11 Nov 1916.

275. Cited in Barton, Secret court martial records, p. 241.

276. Kenneth Griffith and Timothy O'Grady, *Curious journey: an oral history of Ireland's unfinished revolution* (London, 1982), pp 28–36.

277. BMH WS 1019 (Sir Alfred Bucknill), p. 7.

278. Heuston, Headquarters battalion, passim.

279. Cited in Barton, Secret court martial records, p. 258

280. BMH WS 1289 (James Ormond), p.1; BMH WS 1252 (Eamonn Fennell), p. 8.

281. Allen Library, ROI/134.

282. 'Events of Easter Week', *The Catholic Bulletin and Book Review,* vol vi, no. vii (July1916), pp 403–404.

283. Kilmainham Gaol Museum, Heuston papers: 18 PL IC45 24

284. *Wolfe Tone Annual,* 1946, p. 47.

285. Kilmainham Gaol Museum, Heuston papers: MS 21 PL IC45 23

286. Rigney, 'Easter Week 1916 and the Great Southern & Western Railway'; *Yeates, A city in wartime,* p. 174.

Index

16LIVES
JOSEPH PLUNKETT

Honor O Brolchain

O'BRIEN

Joseph Plunkett
16 Lives

by Honor O Brolchain

JOSEPH MARY PLUNKETT, who was born into a wealthy Dublin family in 1887, was a recognised poet, editor of The Irish Review and co-founder of the Irish Theatre. He was also one of the leaders of the 1916 Rising, the designer of the military plan and the youngest signatory of the Proclamation; he joined the IRB, negotiated arms from the German Government and travelled to New York to brief Irish America on the plans for the Rising. By Easter 1916 he was already dying of TB when, aged twenty-eight, he married Grace Gifford in Kilmainham Gaol, just hours before he was executed on 4 May 1916.

Drawing on family archives and Plunkett's personal writings and letters, this is a fascinating, intimate account.

James Connolly
16 Lives

by Lorcan Collins

James Connolly believed in a day when socialism and nationalism would rise together and Ireland would be free of capitalism and imperialism.

Born in Edinburgh in 1868, the son of poor Irish immigrants, James Connolly moved to Dublin in 1896 and founded the Irish Socialist Republican Party and the Workers' Republic newspaper. For seven years he lectured and campaigned for socialism in the US, where he also organised for the Industrial Workers of the World (the Wobblies). In 1913 he stood side by side with Jim Larkin in the fight for workers' rights during the Lockout in Dublin.

A founder of the Irish Citizen Army and sworn into the Irish Republican Brotherhood, he conspired to overthrow British rule in Ireland. He was appointed commandant-general of the army of the Irish Republic and fought in the GPO during the Easter Rising 1916. Despite being severely wounded, Connolly was executed in Kilmainham Gaol on 12 May 1916.

James Connolly's legacy lies in his wealth of socialist writings and his elevation to icon status with his ultimate sacrifice for 'a new society, a new civilisation' for Ireland and her workers.

16LIVES
MICHAEL MALLIN

Brian Hughes

O'BRIEN

Michael Mallin
16 Lives

by Brian Hughes

The first ever series of biographies of the sixteen men executed after the 1916 Easter Rising.

Executed in Kilmainham Gaol on 8 May 1916, Mallin had commanded a garrison of rebels in St Stephen's Green and the College of Surgeons during Easter Week. He was Chief-of-Staff and second-in-command to James Connolly in the Irish Citizen Army. Born in a tenement in Dublin in 1874, he joined the British army aged fourteen as a drummer. He then worked as a silk weaver and became an active trade unionist and secretary of the Silk Weavers' Union.

A devout Catholic, a temperance advocate, father of four young children and husband of a pregnant wife when executed — what brought such a man, with too much to lose, to wage war against the British in 1916?

16 LIVES

EDWARD DALY

Helen Litton

O'BRIEN

Edward Daly

by Helen Litton

Born in Limerick in 1891, John Edward or 'Ned' Daly was the only son in a family of nine. Ned's father, Edward, an ardent Fenian, died before his son was born, but Ned's Uncle John, also a radical Fenian, was a formative influence. John Daly was prepared to use physical force to win Ireland's freedom and was imprisoned for twelve years for his activities. Ned's sister Kathleen married Tom Clarke, a key figure of the Easter Rising. Nationalism was in the Daly blood.

Yet young Ned was seen as frivolous and unmotivated, interested only in his appearance and his social life. How Edward Daly became a professional Volunteer soldier, dedicated to freeing his country from foreign rule, forms the core of this biography.

Drawing on family memories and archives, Edward Daly's grandniece Helen Litton uncovers the untold story of Edward Daly, providing an insight into one of the more enigmatic figures of the Easter Rising.

As commandant during the Rising, Ned controlled the Four Courts area. On 4 May 1916, Commandant Edward Daly was executed for his part in the Easter Rising. Ned was twenty-five years old. His body was consigned to a mass grave.